The Red Fox Family

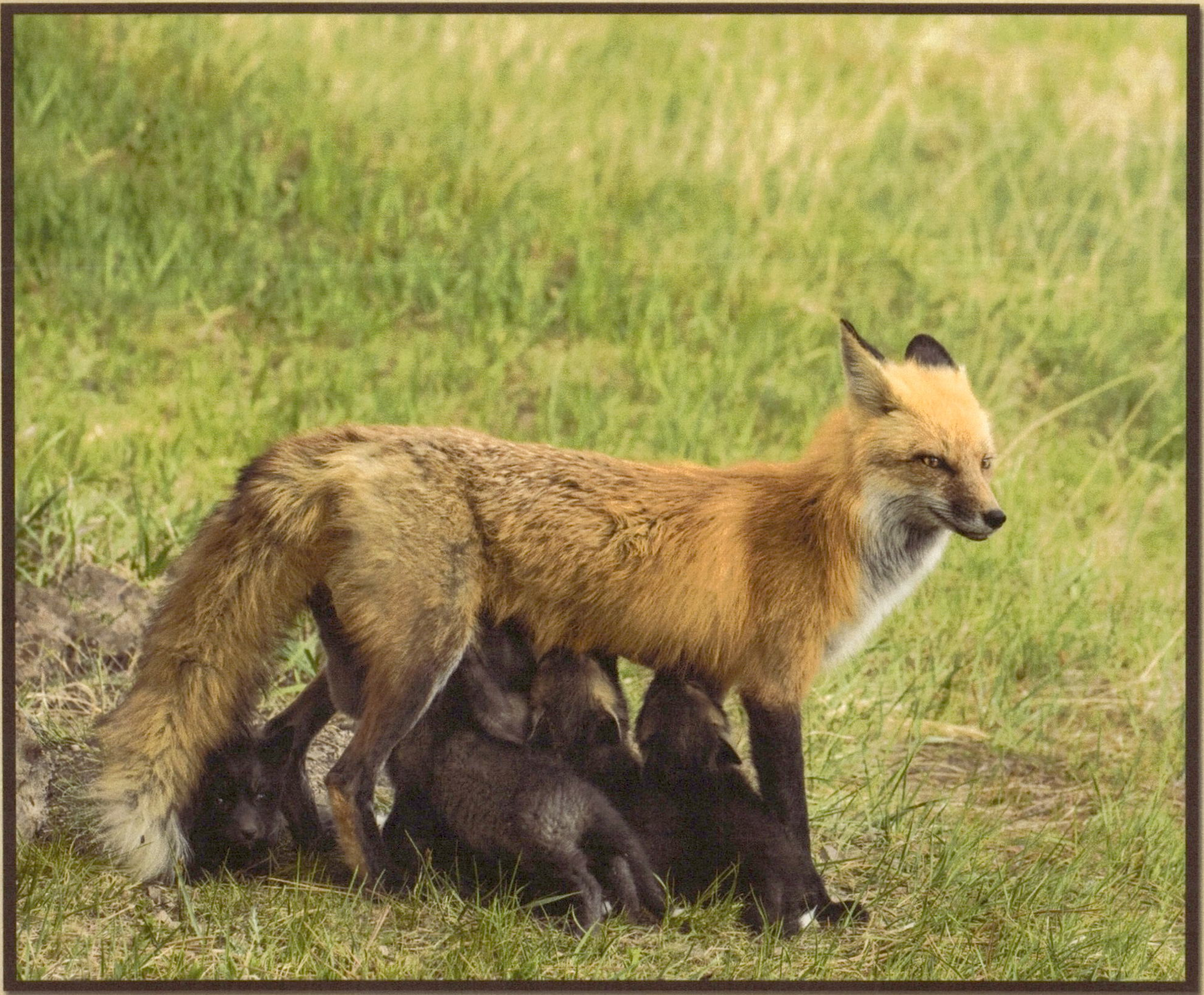

Lois Lake

Copyright 2015 by Lois Lake

Published 2015.

Printed in the United States of America.

Photographs by Lois Lake.

ISBN 978-1-943650-02-6

Library of Congress Control Number 2015947236

Published by BookCrafters, Parker Colorado.

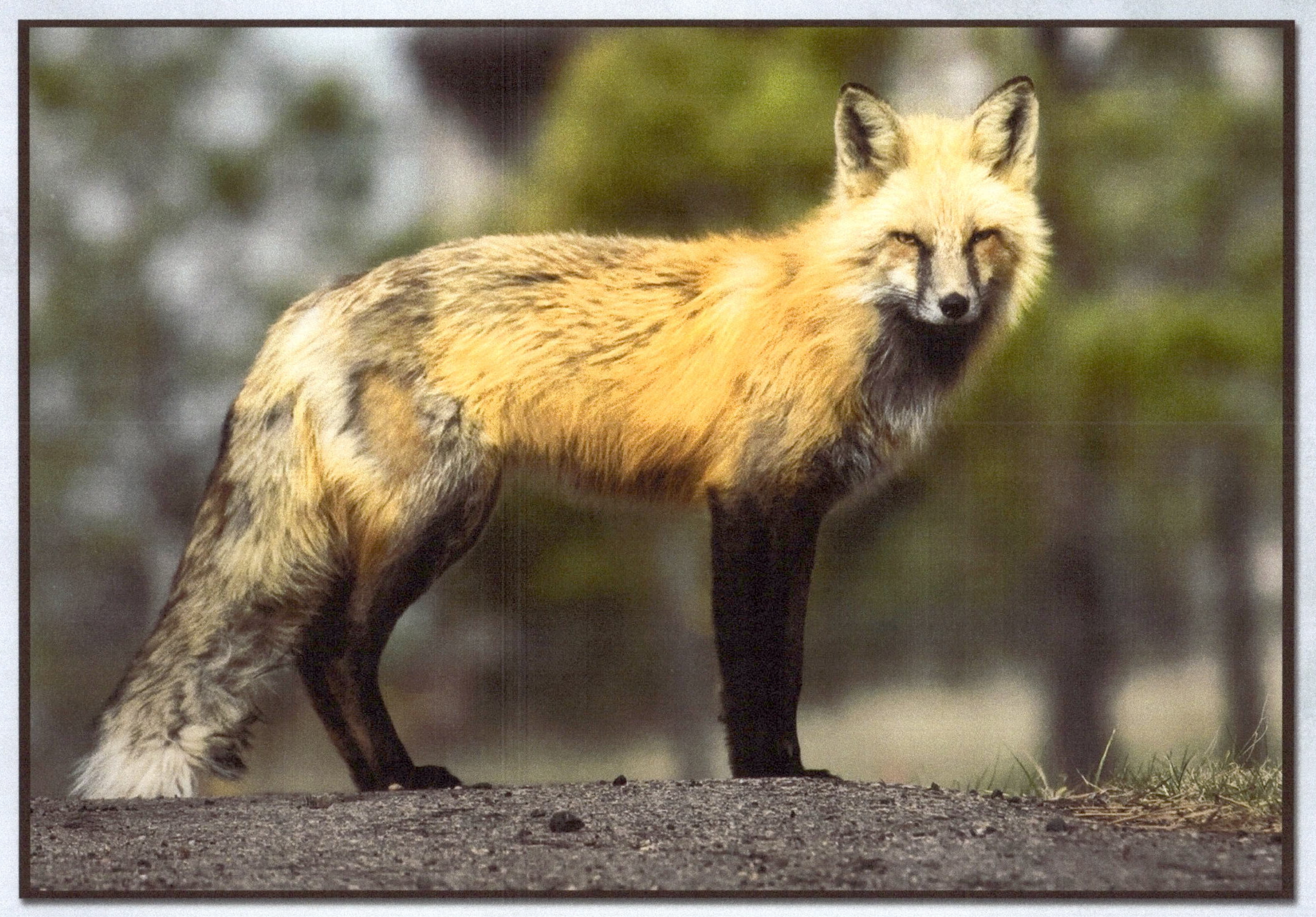

This book is dedicated to Loyceine Grier who graciously allowed me to hang out on her property hours at a time, day after day, just hoping to have the opportunity to capture an image of the red fox kits. After many days and a lot of hours patiently waiting, I finally got to see the kits, but the journey of waiting for them is a story worth telling as well. Thank you Loyceine! You have given me an opportunity that very few photographers get in their lifetime.

The red fox is the largest of the fox species. They can be found all across the Northern Hemisphere. They make their home in the suburbs as well as rural areas. They are well known for their ability to adapt to their environment.

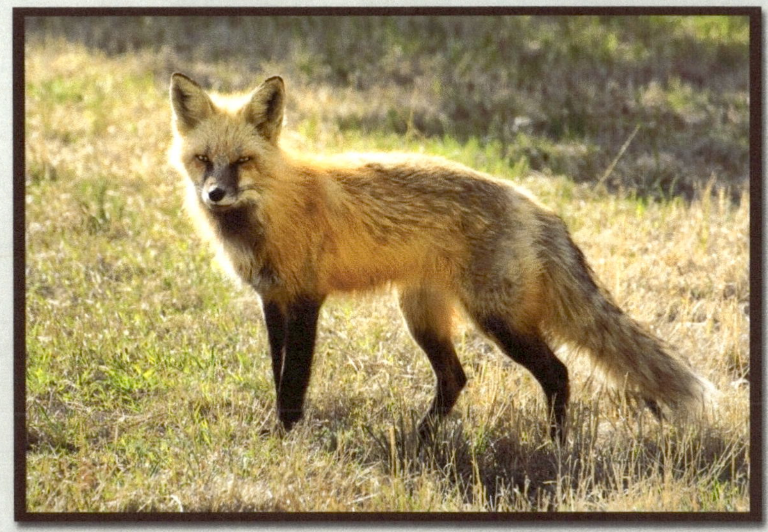

They have the unique ability to find any little space that is suitable for a den. The male is called a "dog," the female is called a "vixen," and the babies are called "kits." The male is slightly larger than the female. Their primary food source is mice, voles, squirrels and rabbits.

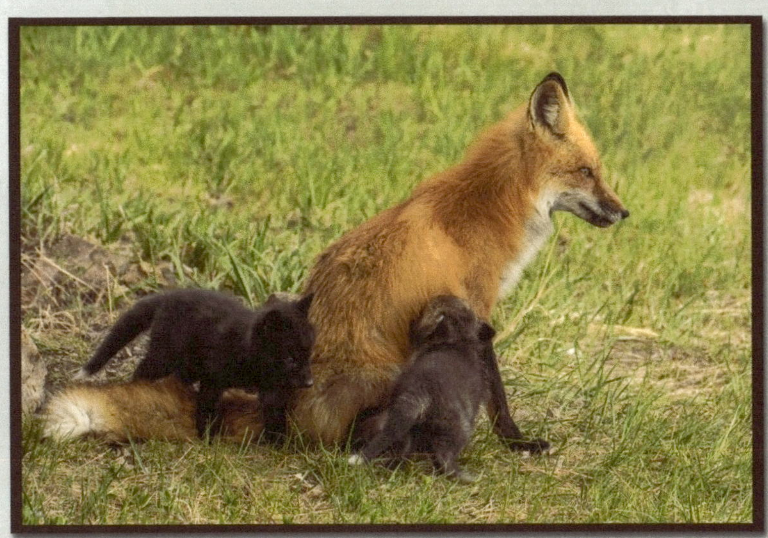

Sometimes you will see them cock their head to the side listening for mice or voles burrowing underground. Then you will see them jump into the air and pounce on their prey with extreme accuracy.

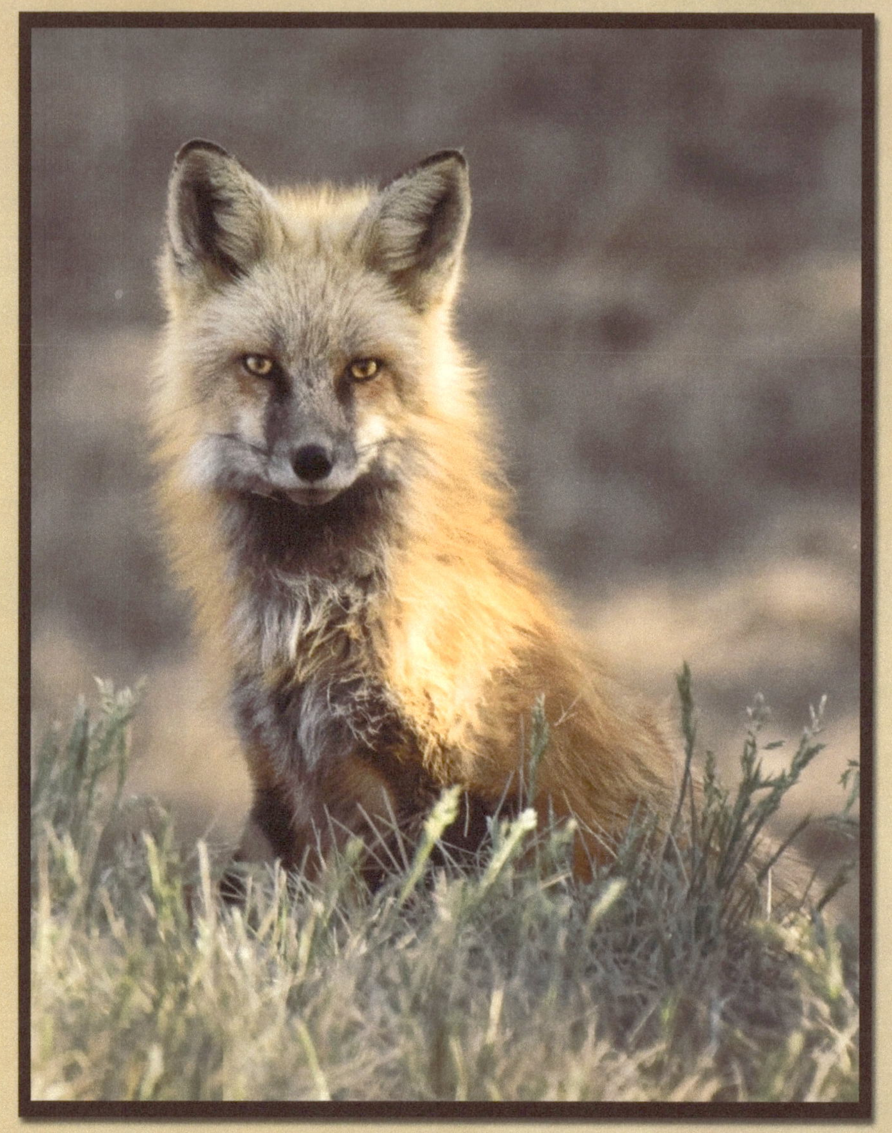

A couple of years ago I was told about a red fox den. Sometimes animals will return to their birthing places year after year so I thought I would see if the red fox came back to the den again this year. I was excited to see the male fox sitting near the road as I drove by. It ran out through the pasture so I decided to park nearby and watch to see what happened. It was not long until I saw it just over the ridge quietly watching me.

I returned the next day to see if the kits were coming out of the den yet. When I arrived, the male fox was lying out in the pasture taking a nap. It immediately got up and watched me for a while and then it sat down to scratch and yawned. After about an hour it went around toward the road so I thought it went hunting. The next thing I know it is sitting on the other side of me just watching. It circled around both sides of the car and in front of it checking to determine if I was a threat.

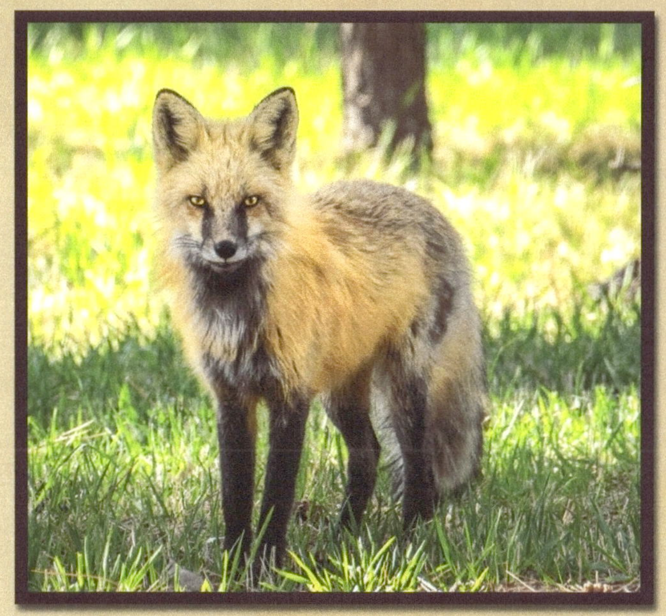

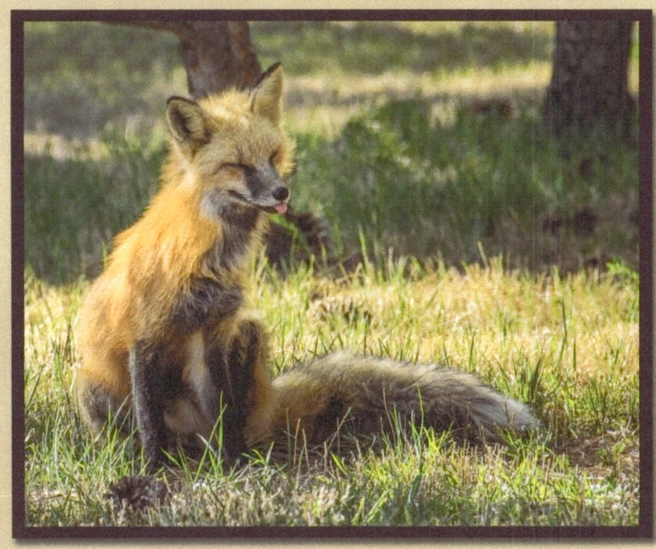

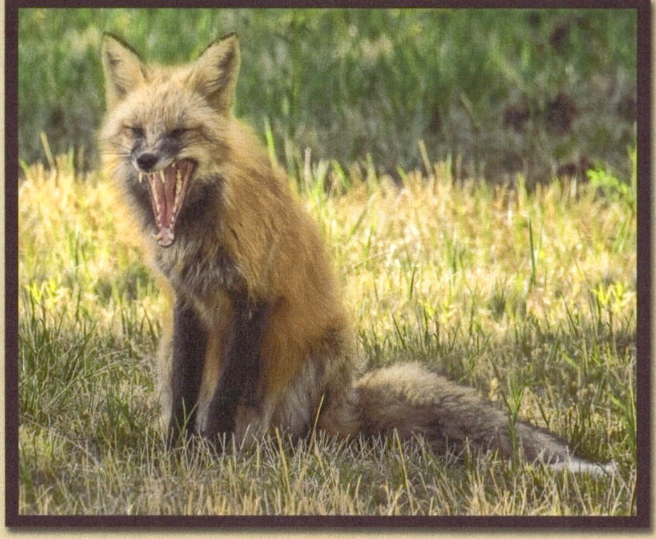

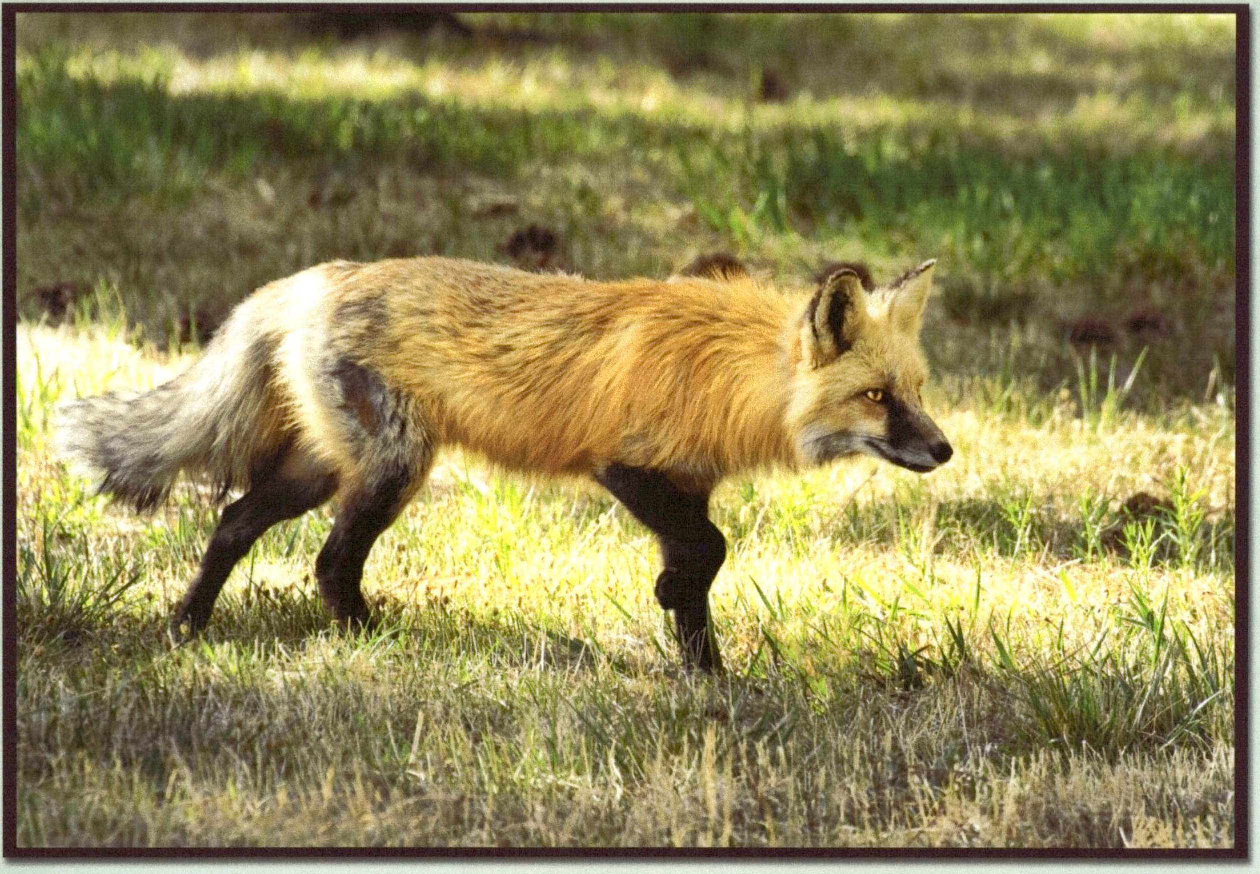

Each day when I arrived at the den
the male fox was not far away. It
appeared to be taking a nap, but it
was always aware of any activity in
the area. As I waited, I could hear
the squirrels playing and chattering
and scampering about. Always at a
safe distance; or at least I thought.
Suddenly, something changed. The
male fox was on his feet and in full
hunting mode.

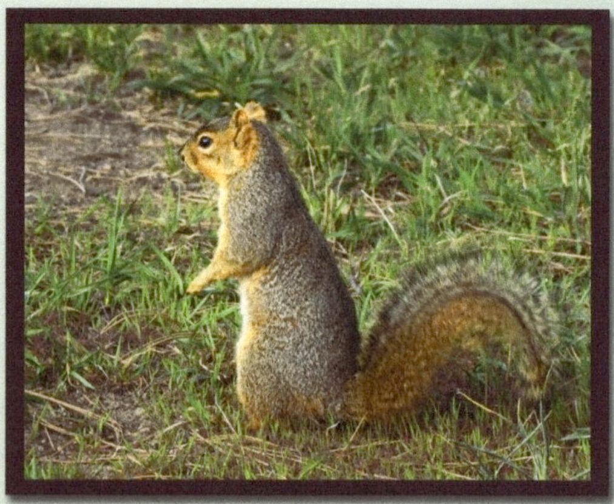

One day I arrived just in time to see the male fox go hunting. As I was waiting for him to return, I caught a movement out of the corner of my eye. Another adult fox came out of the den and was stretching as they do after a nap. I raised my camera to get a shot and it spooked her. She woofed at me and immediately disappeared into the den again. Up to this point in time I was not sure that there were kits in the den. Now I knew the female adult was in the den with kits and the male was out hunting for dinner.

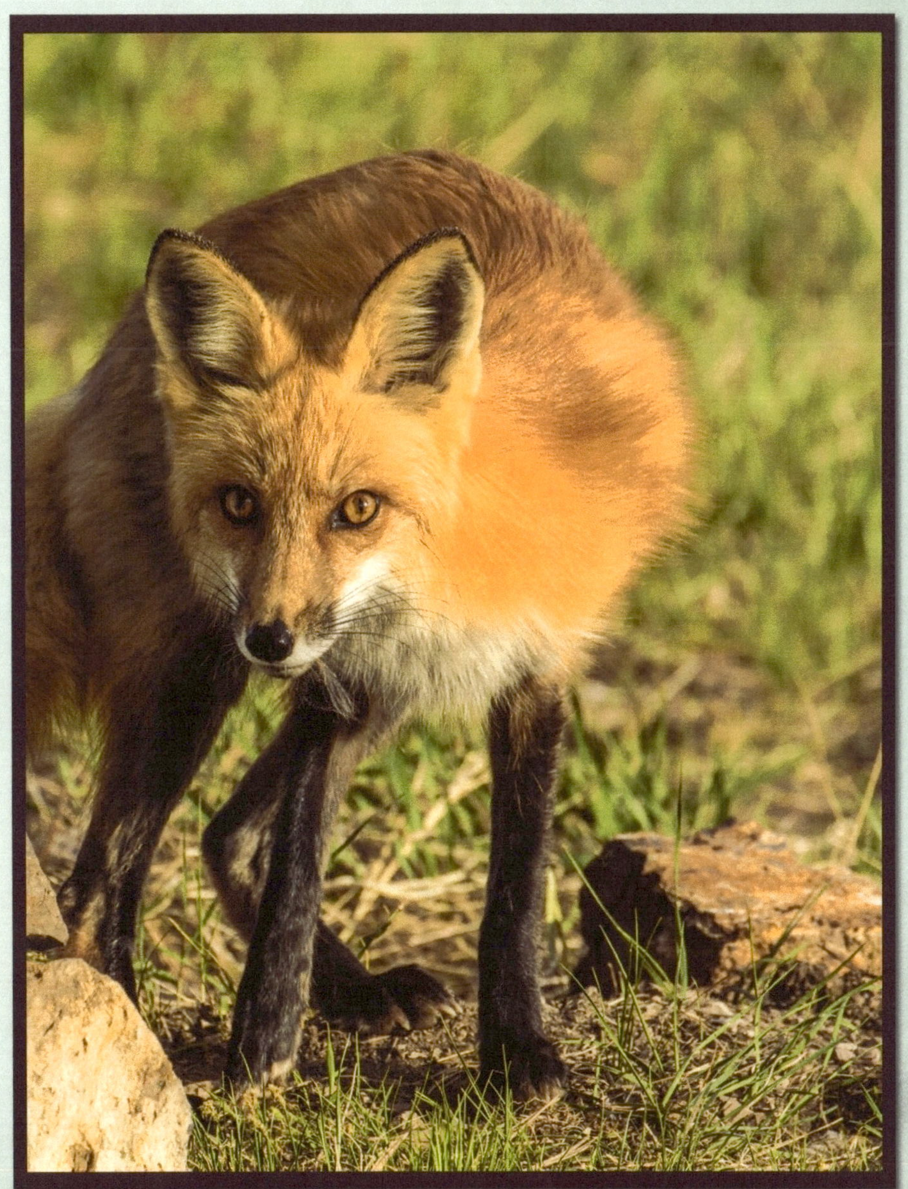

I saw the male fox circling around behind a tree. It brought a vole back to feed the female, but it did not approach the den. Instead, it buried the vole about twenty feet from the tree and then disappeared into the gully.

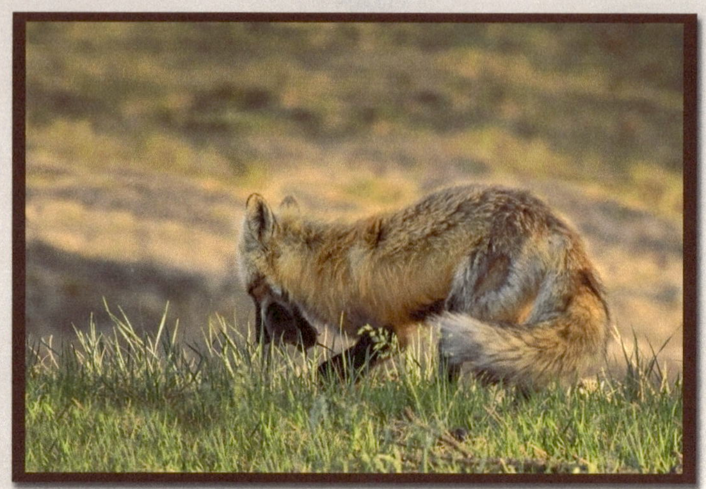

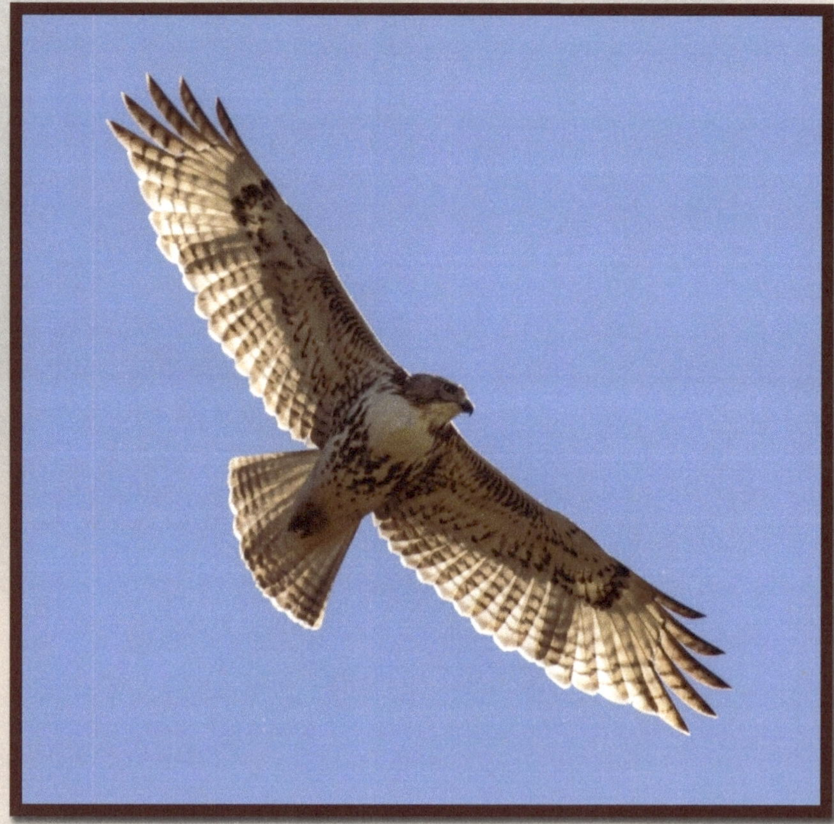

As I waited and watched, I saw two large red-tailed hawks circling just above the trees. I started paying closer attention and then I heard a baby red-tailed hawk squawking for food.

It made me wonder if the red-tailed hawk saw the fox bury its prey in the pasture and they would rob its cache.

One afternoon I saw the vixen come
to the den. She quietly sat down and
surveyed the surrounding area for
danger. After determining that it was
safe, she made a low, guttural noise
in her throat which was a signal to
the kits that it was safe to come
out of the den. After eleven days of
watching the den, finally, the kits
came out.

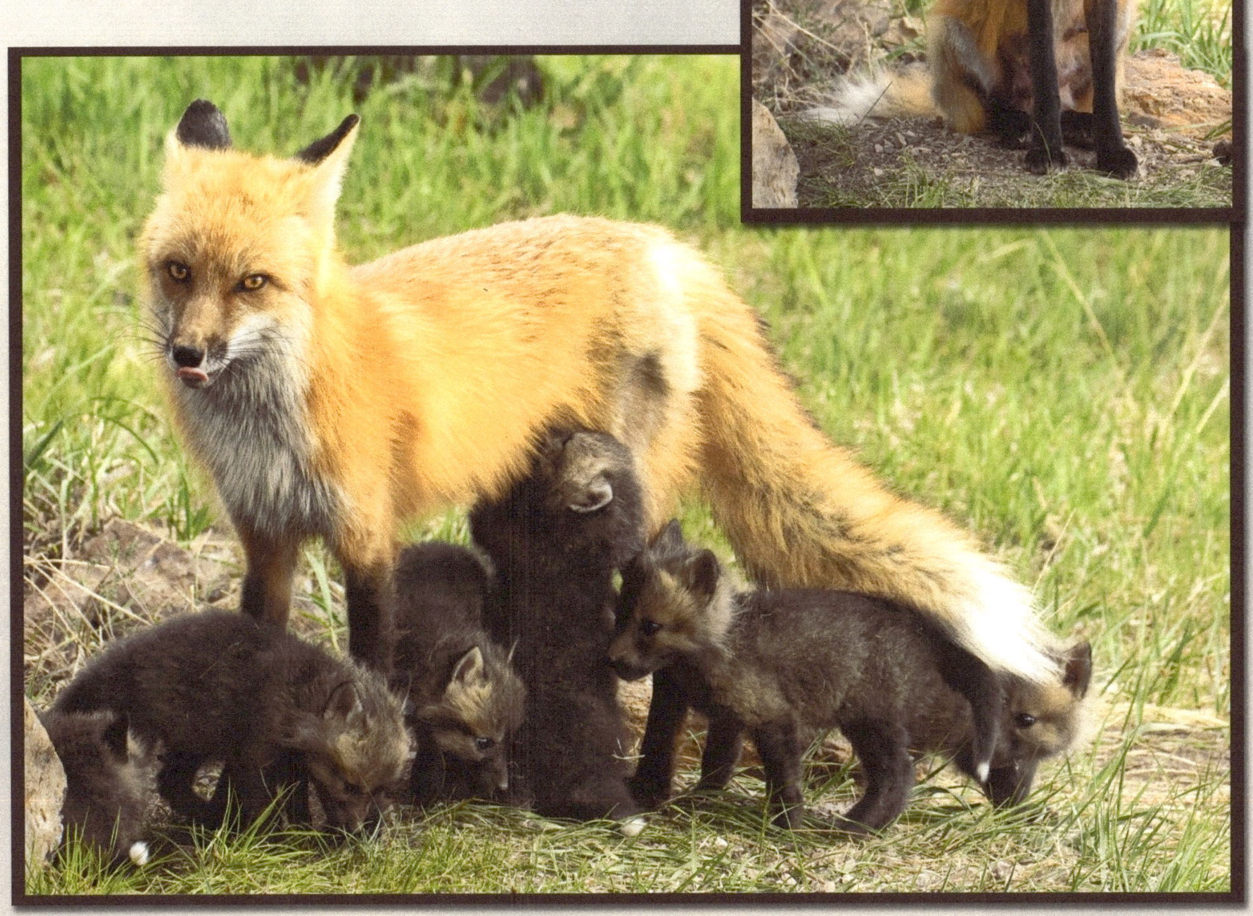

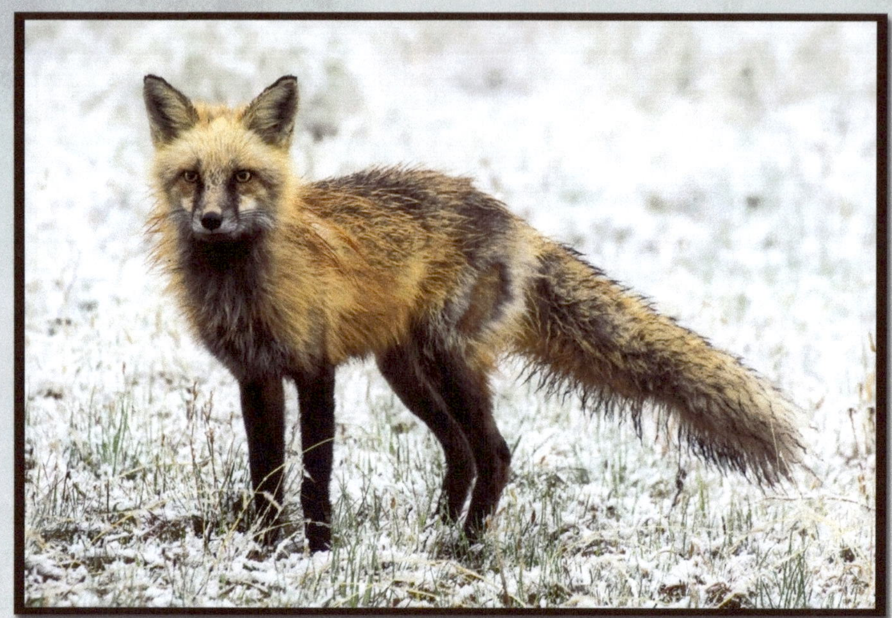

It was thirty-three degrees with snow on the ground and fog in the air this morning when I arrived at the fox den. As I approached I saw the adult fox with his fur wet and cold. I marveled at the skills it must take to survive the elements of winter.

Not long after the fox went hunting, I counted nineteen head of deer coming up out of the gully and into the pasture. All of a sudden the herd of deer charged. I looked in the direction they were going and saw that they were charging the fox. The deer chased the fox up and over the hill as far away as I could see. Deer and fox are natural enemies because the deer are afraid the fox will get their babies.

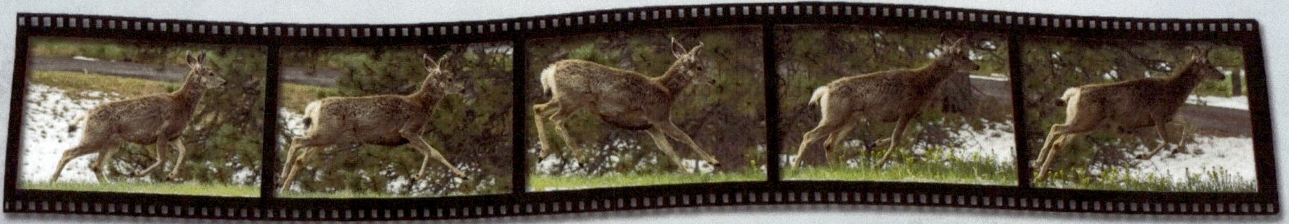

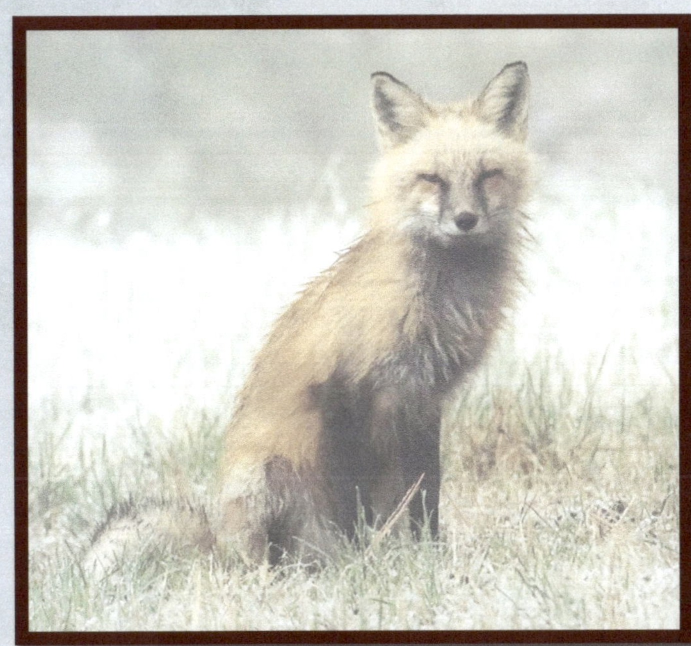

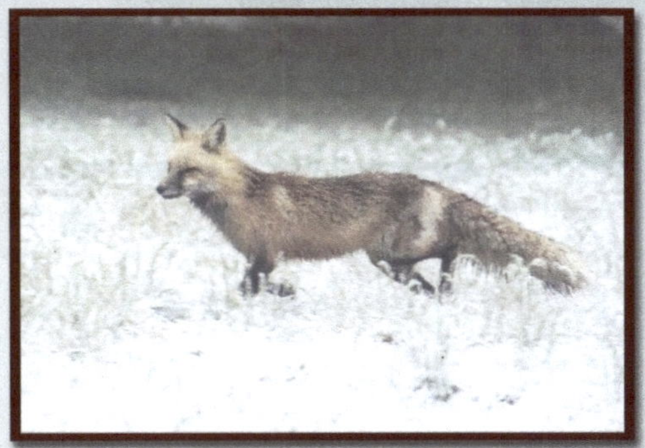

Before long I saw the vixen return with a rabbit in her mouth. She had been hunting in the tall, wet grass. She was soaking wet from the tip of her nose to the tip of her tail. Rain or shine, wind or snow; the kits must be fed.

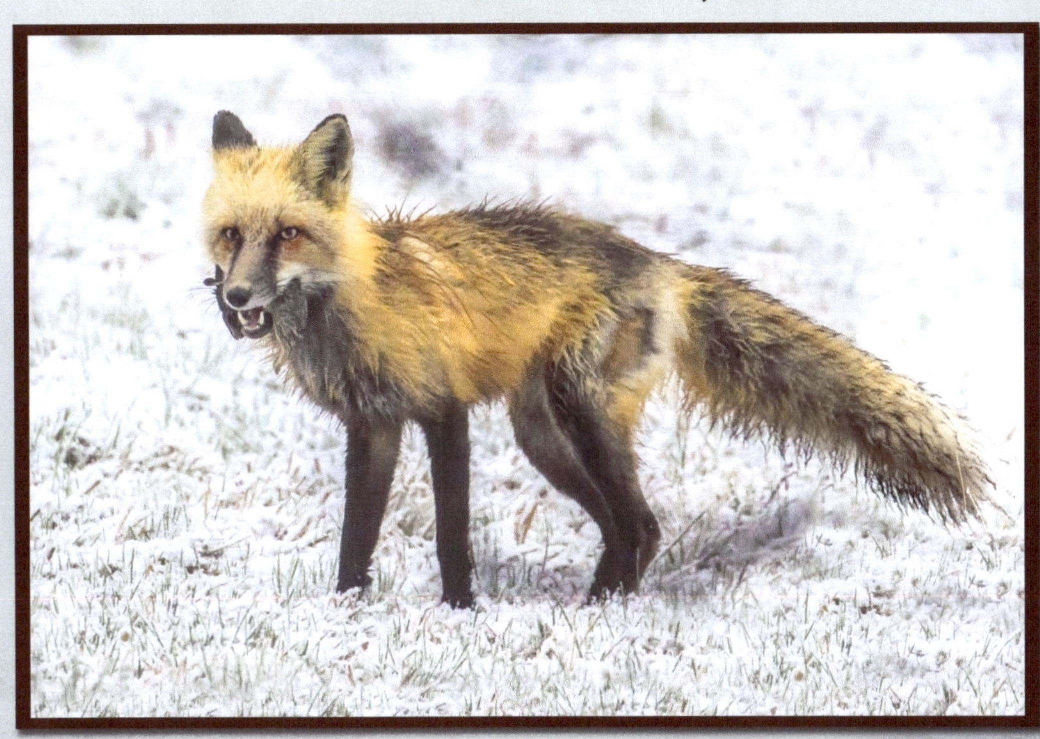

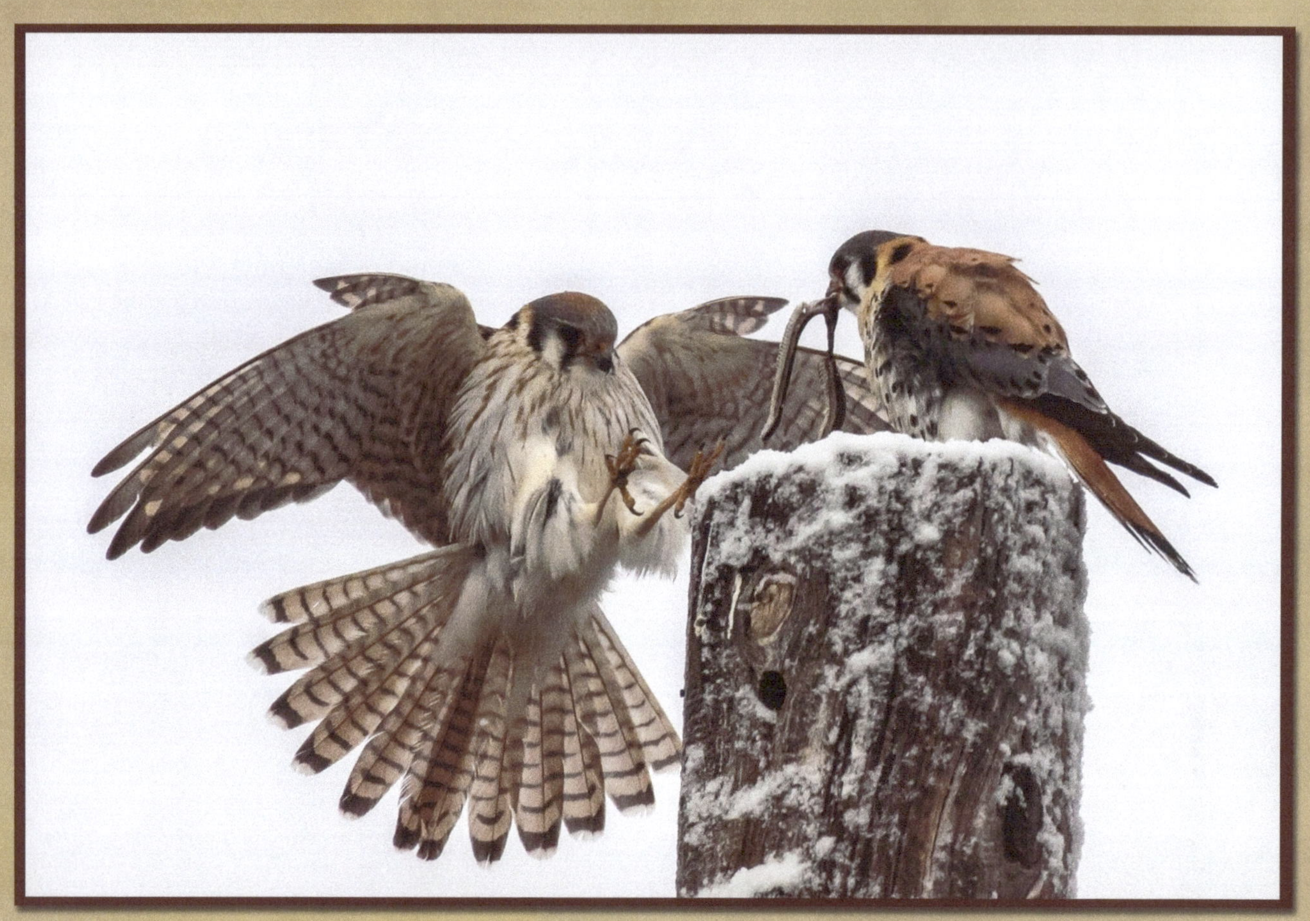

I wondered if the kits would come out in this weather or if they would stay tucked in the den where it was warm. As I watched, I saw the male kestrel flying toward me with a snake in its mouth. He gave the cry, cry, cry to announce that he had food and began tearing bits off the snake and eating. The female kestrel came in to join him and they dined together for some time and then they flew off to the top of a tree and I could hear the coo, coo, coo as they mated. This behavior is called courtship feeding.

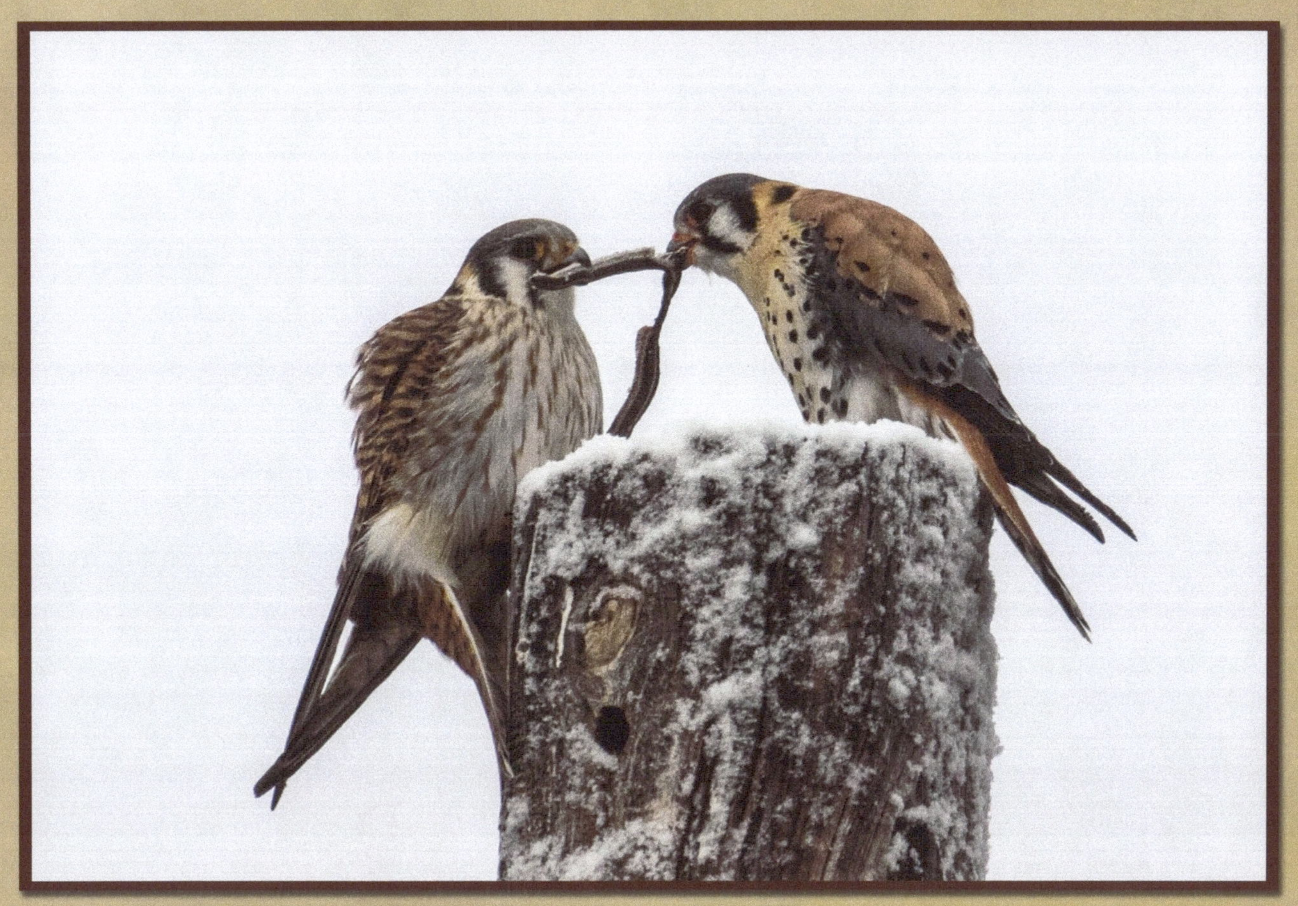

I sat there and wondered where the kestrel found a snake in the snow. I thought snakes were cold-blooded creatures and hibernated in the winter. I guess with the temperature being in the 60 degree range one day and in the 30 degree range the next day the snakes were confused as to whether it was winter or summer.

I saw the vixen returning to the den with something in her mouth. It was hard to tell what it was because there were legs sticking out every direction. As she got closer, I was able to tell she had three mice in her mouth. She deposited the food in the den and then came back out and just sat there.

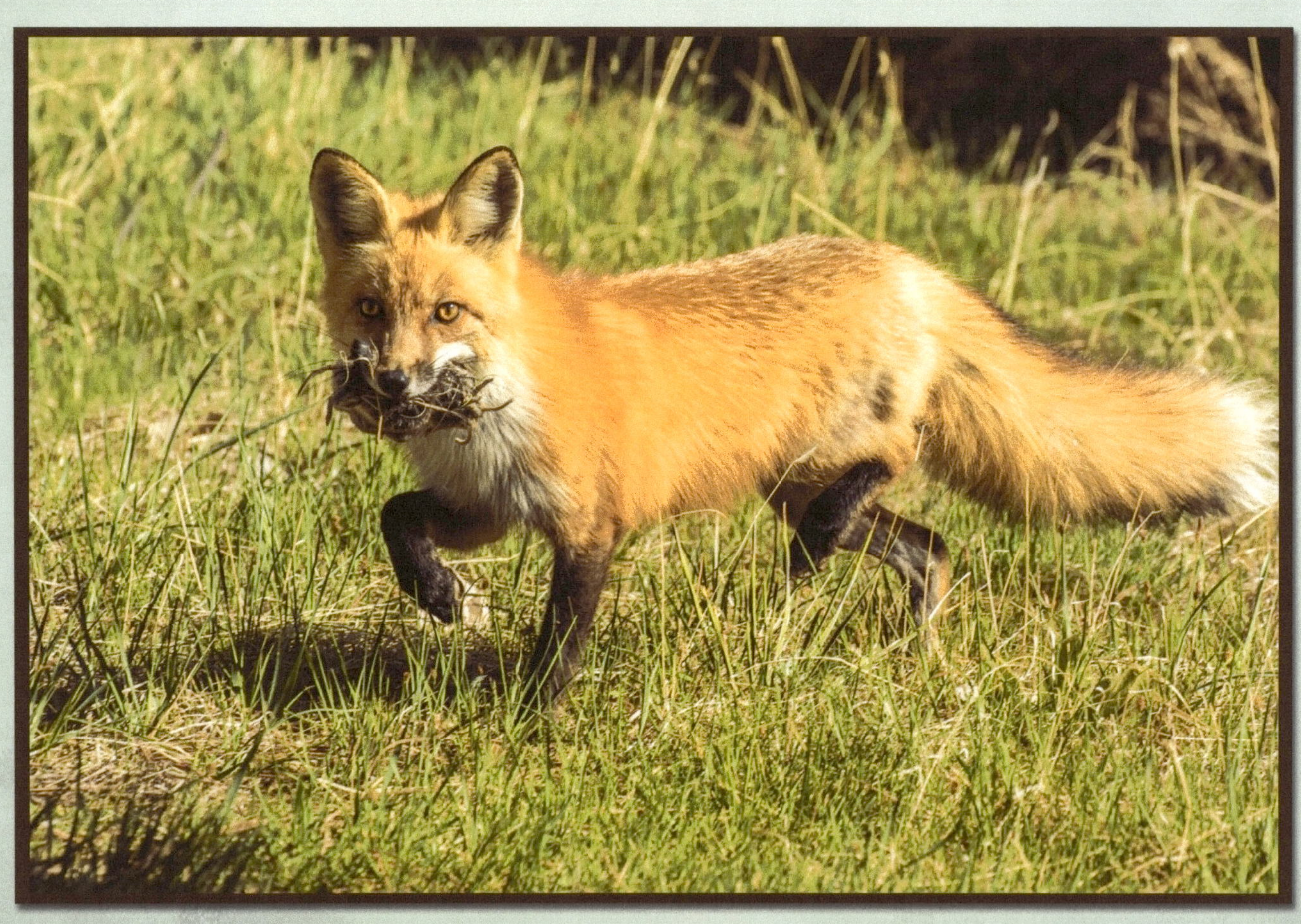

After a few minutes I heard her mew to the kits telling them it was safe to come out and play. Fox kits came out from both the north and south entrance of the den. I counted as they came out expecting to see five or six kits, but they kept coming. I counted ten kits. I could not believe my eyes so I counted again and again. I thought perhaps they were moving so fast that I had miscounted, but each time that I counted I came up with ten kits. I could not help but wonder if all of these kits belong to one vixen or if it is a combined family.

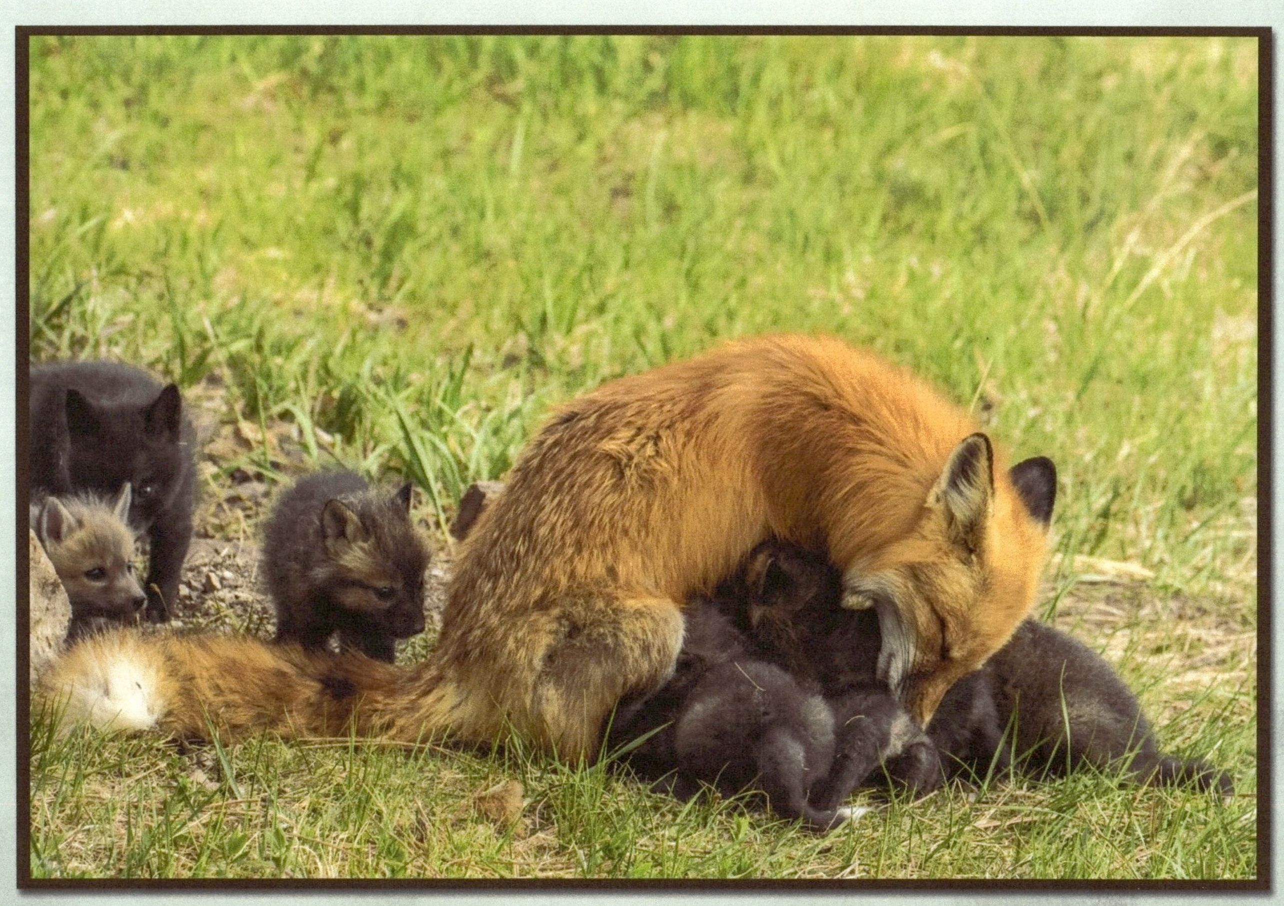

Not all of the kits could nurse at the same time. They had to take turns. At first she sat down while nursing them and then she stood up so more of the kits could have easier access to nurse.

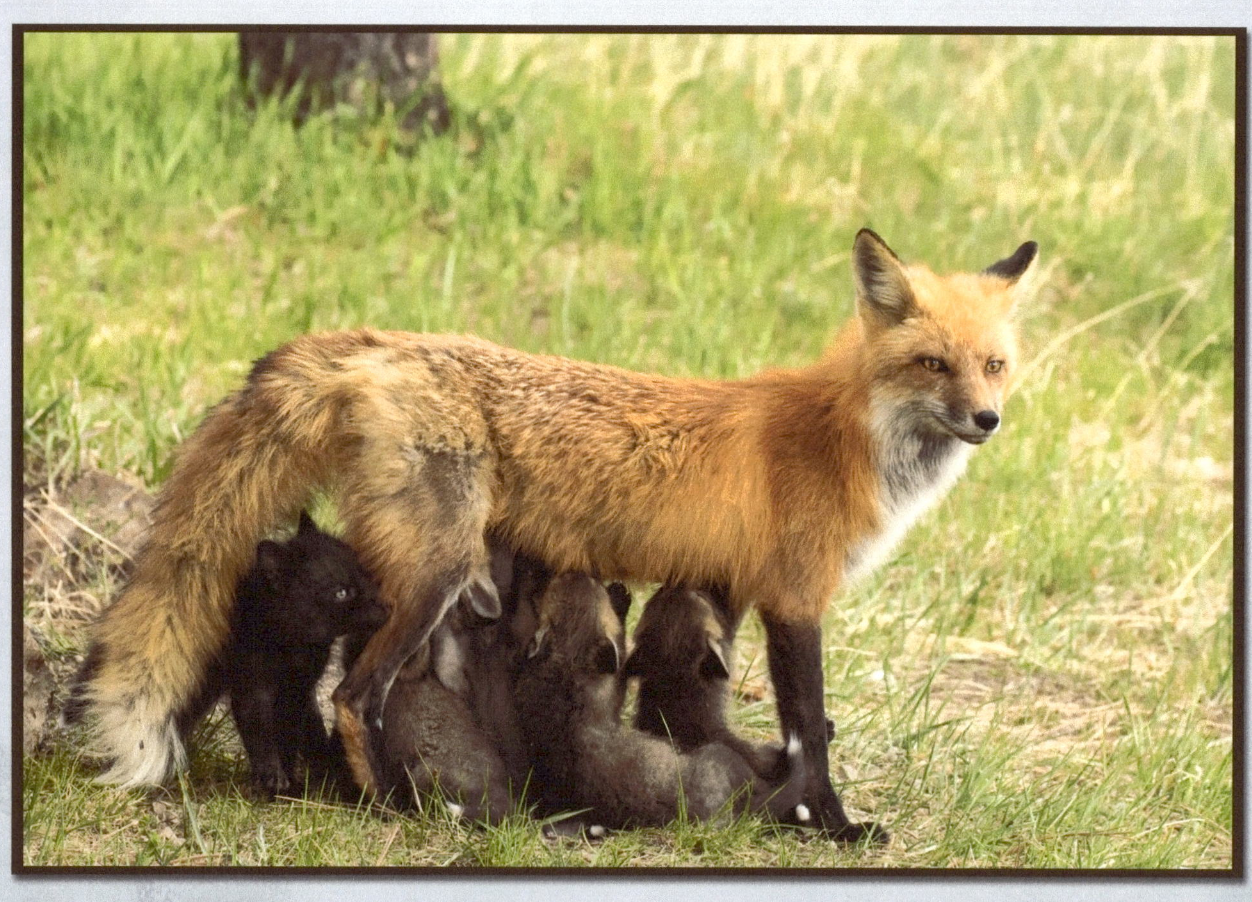

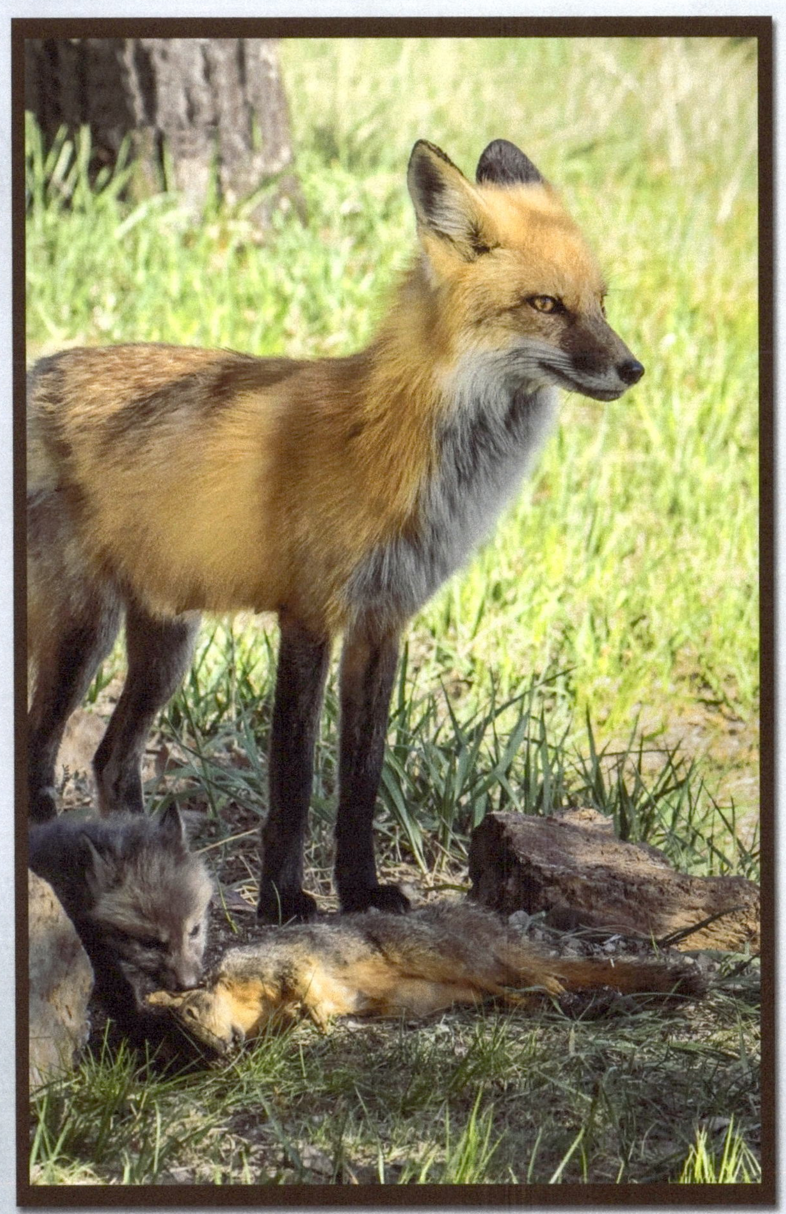

One day the vixen came out of the den, sat down and looked around to make sure all was safe. She went from the south entrance of the den to the north entrance and pulled out a dead squirrel. She took it and laid it directly in front of the entrance to the den. I heard her make that guttural noise telling the kits it was safe to come out, but she would not nurse the kits until they crawled over the dead squirrel. The kits spent some time getting familiar with the dead squirrel, pulling it around and then the vixen let them nurse. I wondered if this was her way of introducing solid foods to supplement the nursing.

One afternoon while the vixen
was nursing, all of a sudden,
the vixen woofed and all ten
kits scrambled for shelter
immediately. I looked around
to see what the danger was
and I saw the deer charging
the male fox again.

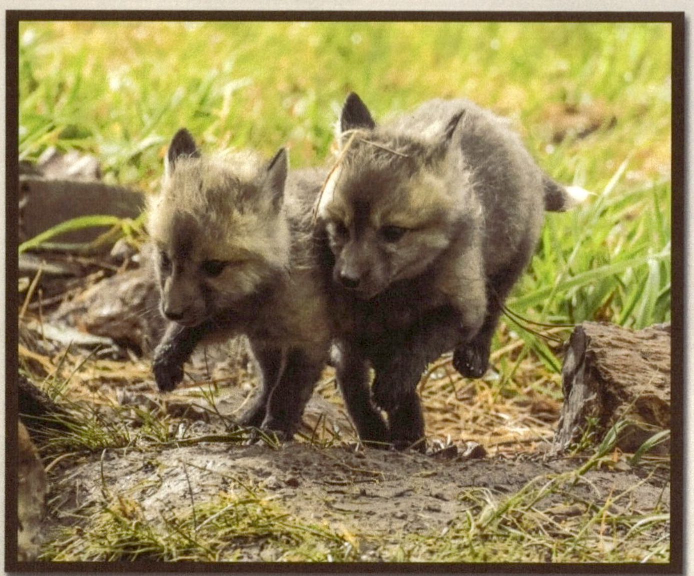

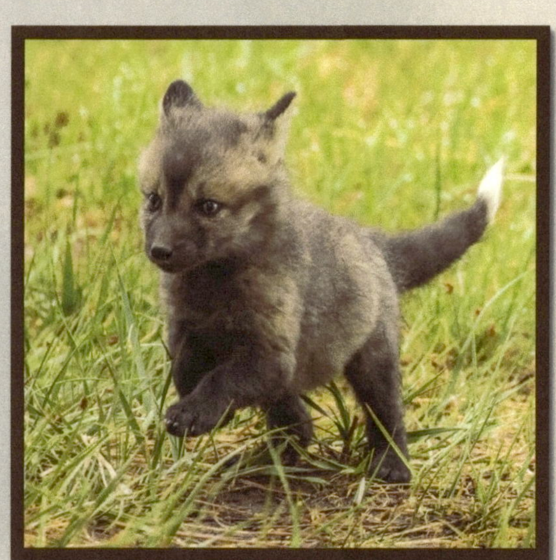

He circled away from the
den and tried to lead the
deer away. A few deer
followed, but a couple
of the deer continued
to approach the den. The
vixen followed the kits
into the den to keep
them safe.

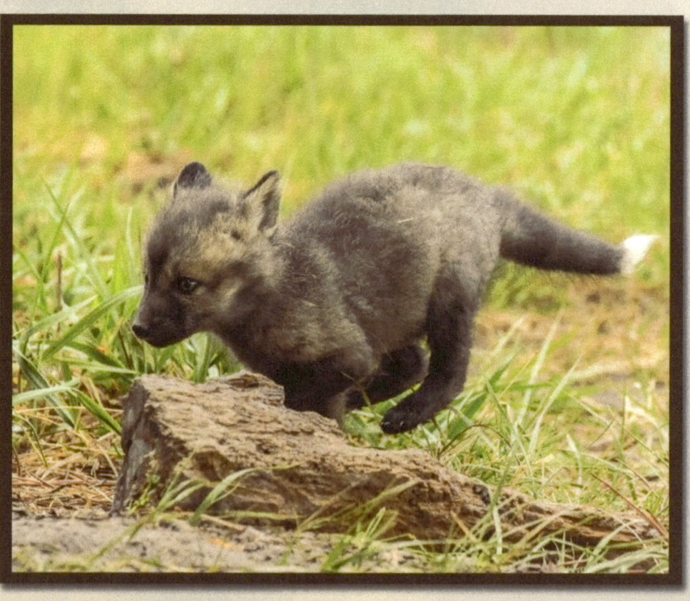

The deer was curious so it came closer and closer to the den.
The kits were curious also. I saw two of the kits peek out of
the den. The deer was not more than five feet away. I wished
I had a way to warn the kits about the hooves of deer. Their
instinct must have taken over because it wasn't long before
the kits disappeared back into the den and the deer lost
interest and browsed on over the ridge.

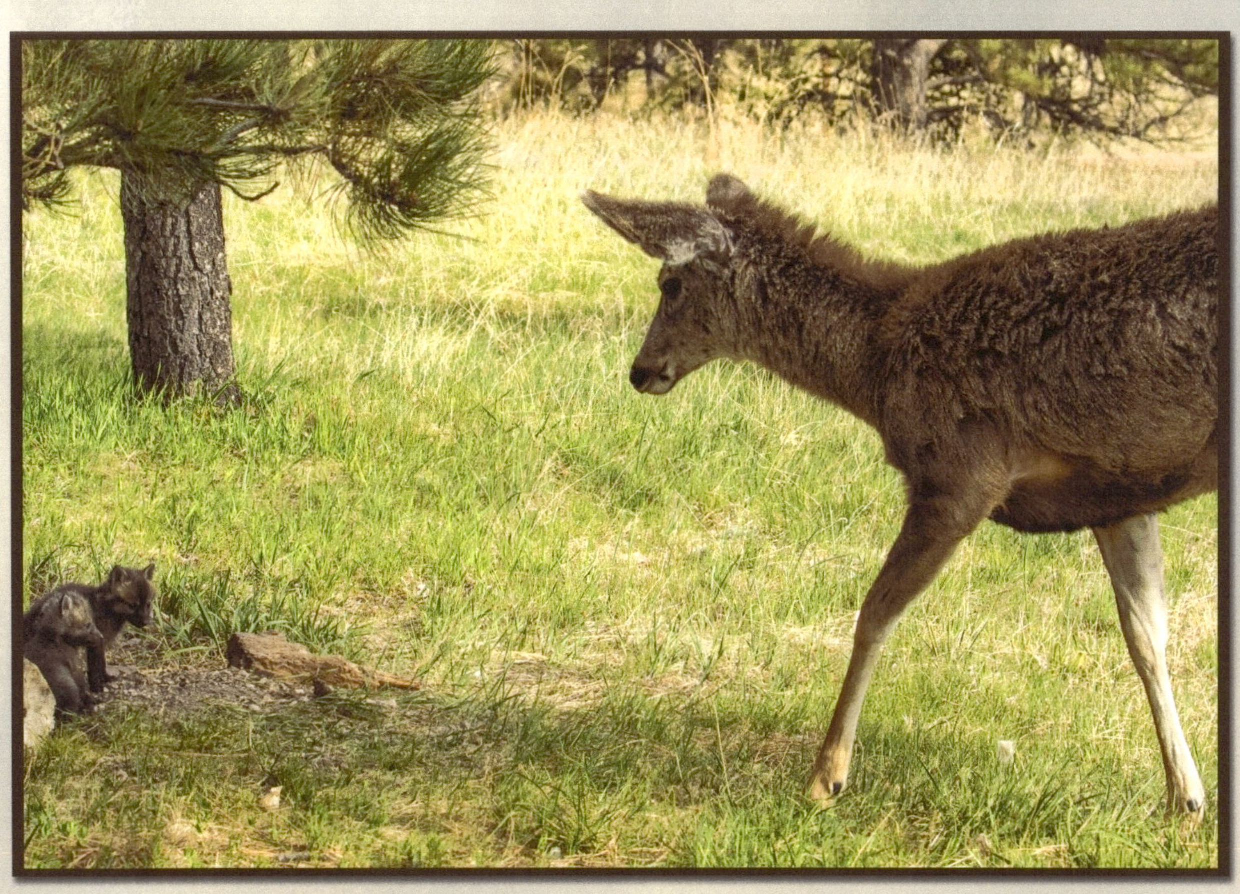

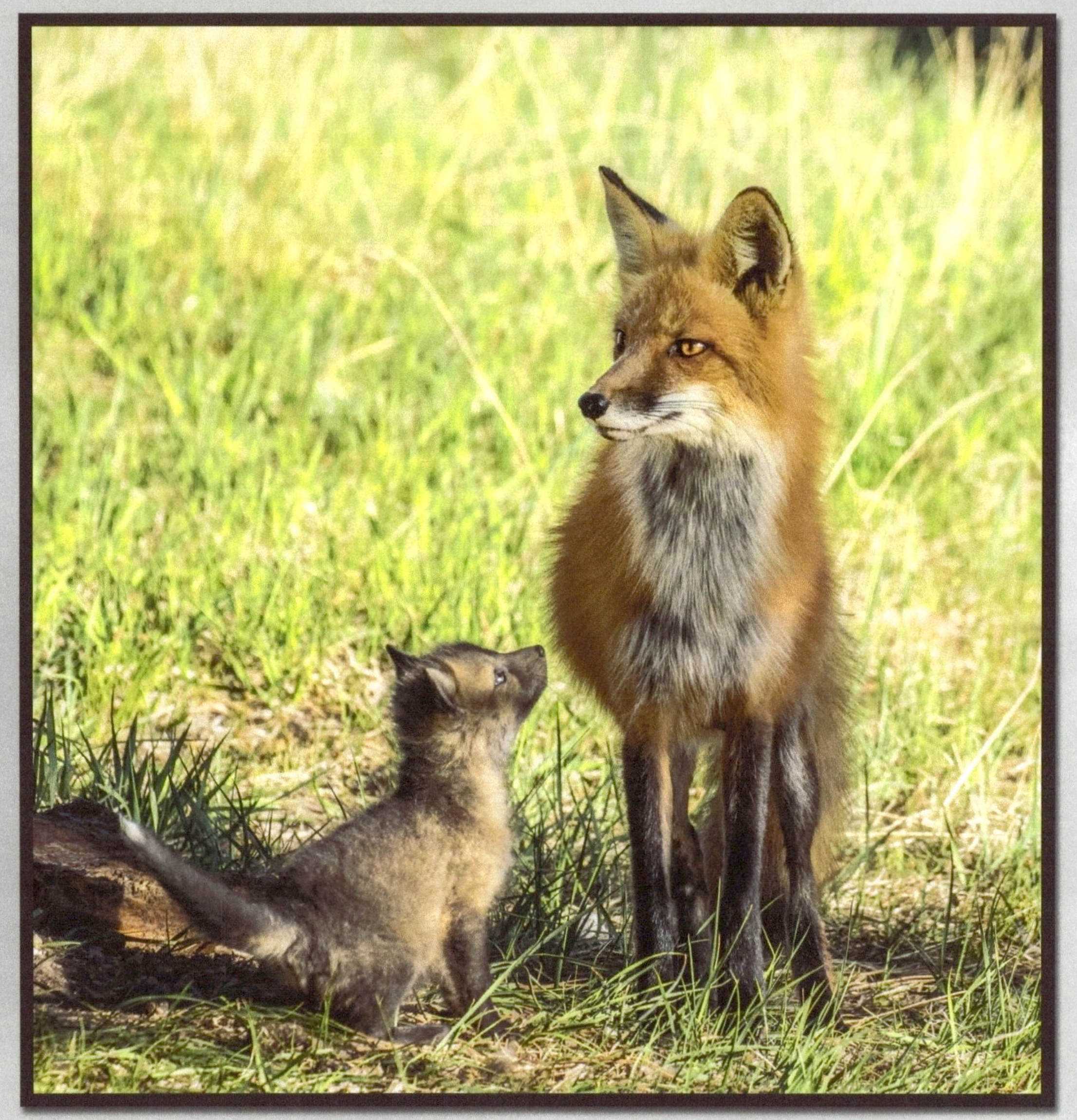

Each day I watched as the kits grew bigger and ventured a little farther from the den. It was amazing to me that in all the time that I spent at the den waiting for the vixen to return or waiting for the kits to come out to play, (and I spent a lot of hours watching), the kits never came out of the den until the vixen told them it was safe.

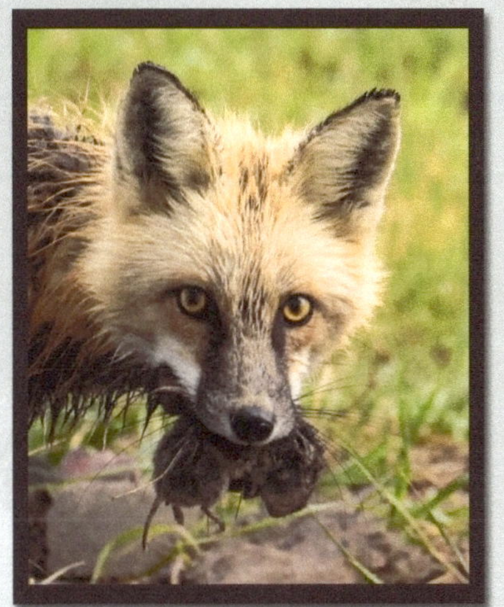

One evening as the vixen stopped at the south entrance to the den she called the kits with her low, guttural voice. The kits all came running out. The vixen dropped a mouse and several kits scrambled to get it. One kit that was more aggressive than the others got the mouse and ran away with it. The other kits chased after it. I could see their hunting skills starting to develop.

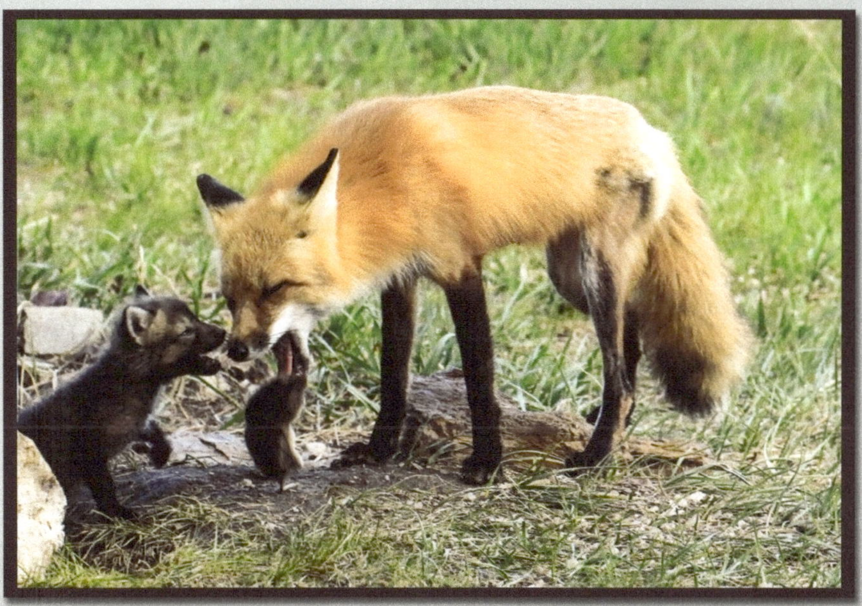

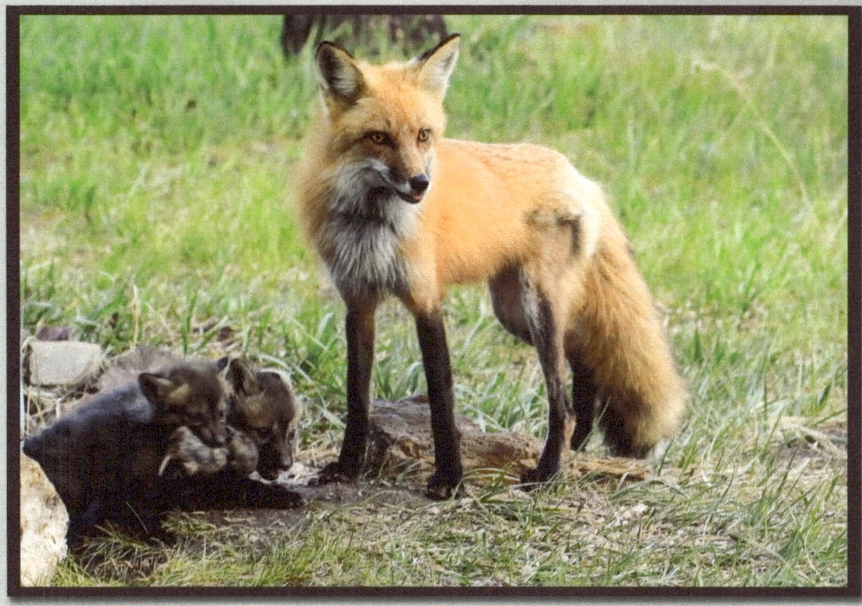

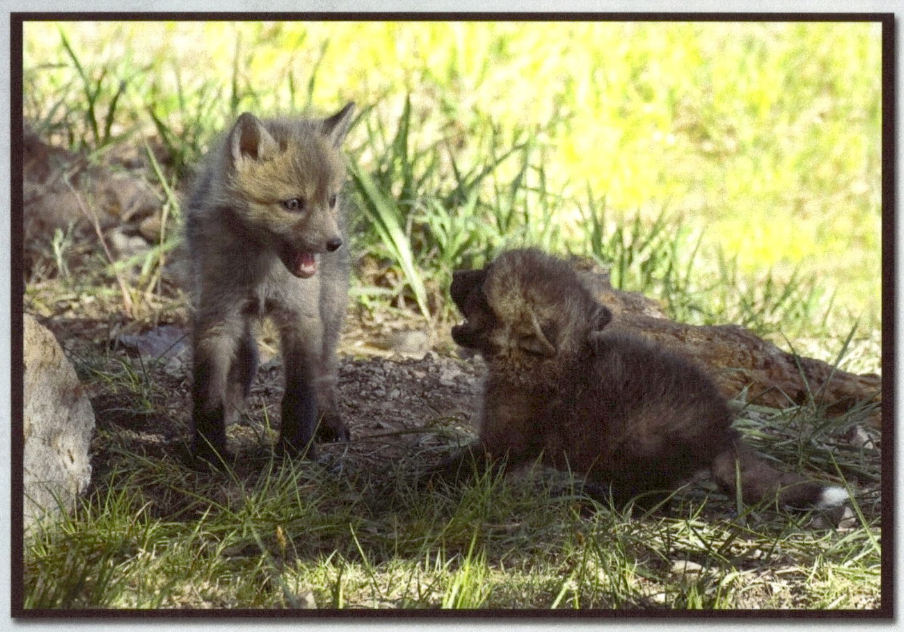

The kits began
to develop
personalities.
Some became
the attacker
and others
the defender.

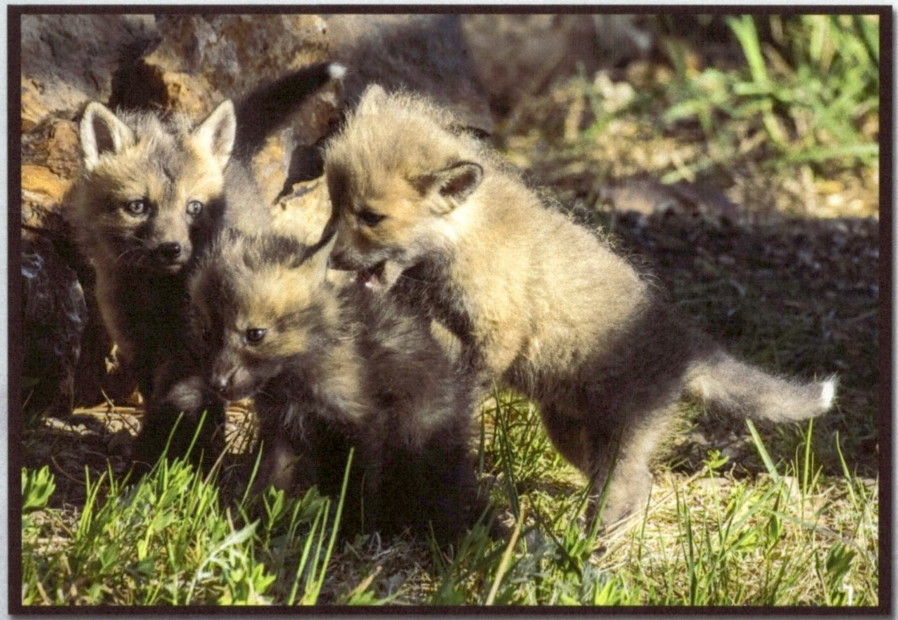

It looked like
they were
playing a game
of tag, but
really they were
developing skills
of cooperation
for the hunt.

As the fox kits grew, so did their curiosity. They began to venture farther and farther from the den. Insects are relatively easy to catch and can be a major portion of the kit's diet as they learn to hunt on their own.

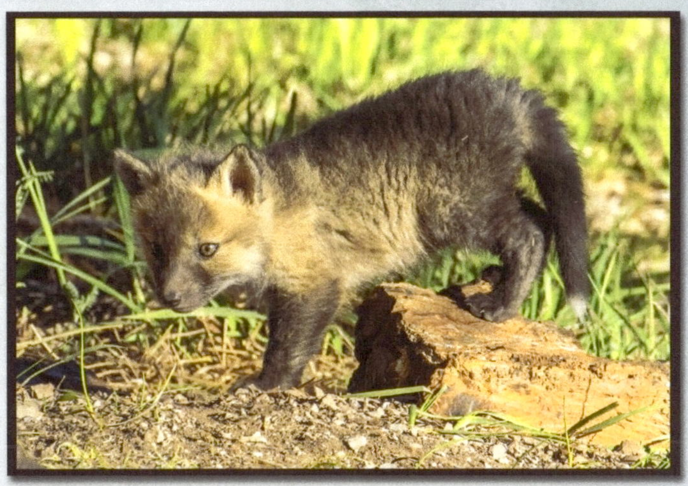

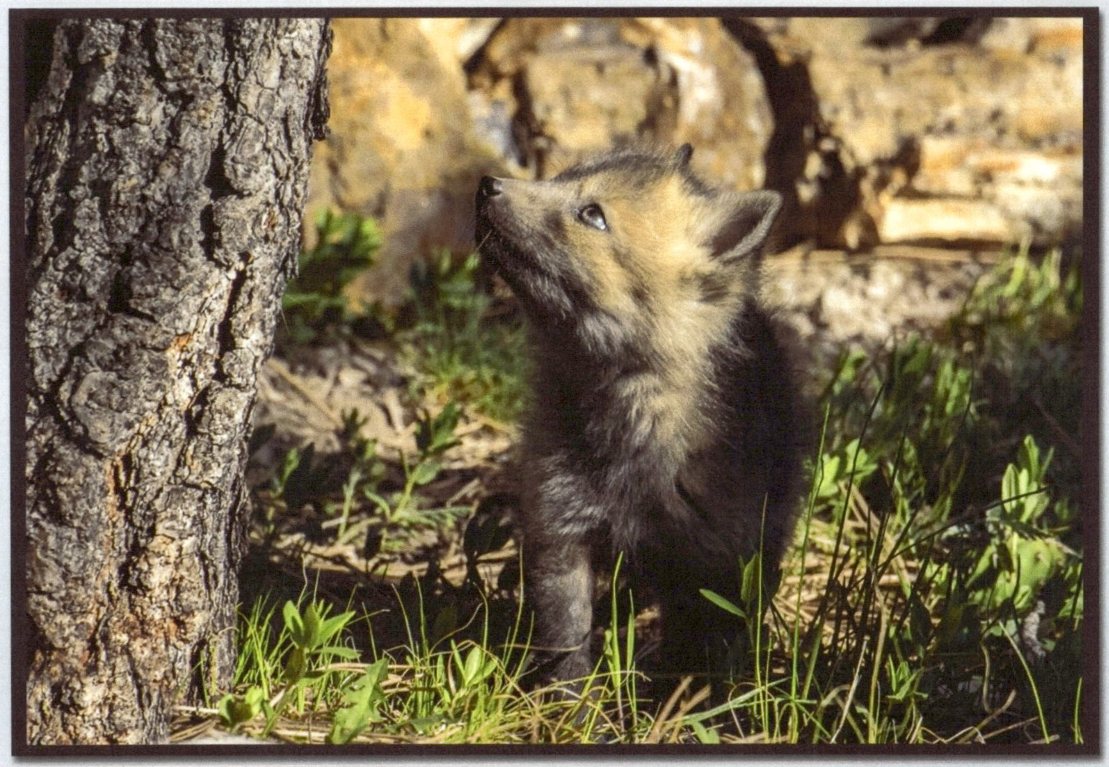

Their awareness expanded beyond each other and things on the ground to things above them.

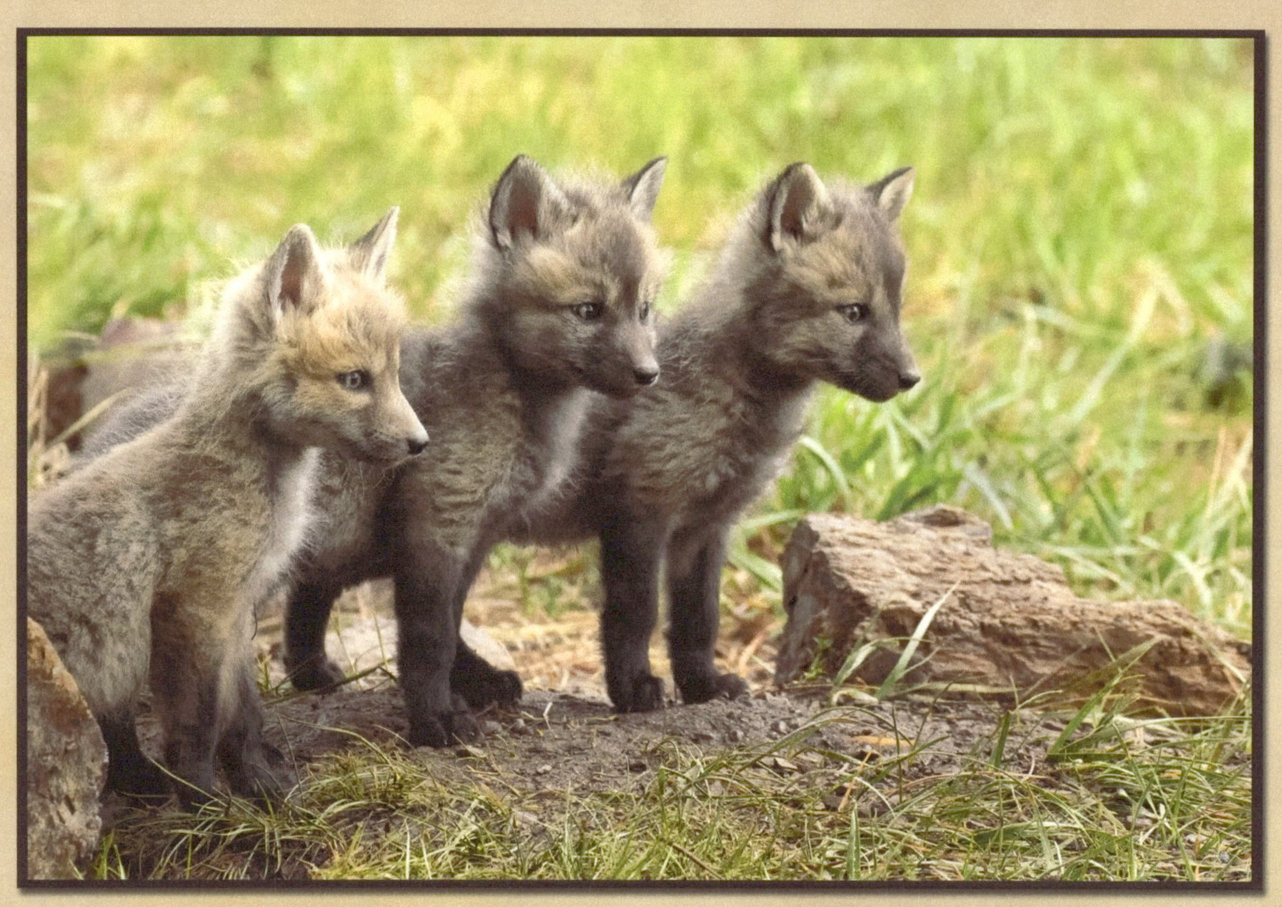

Three fox kits came out of the den.
Something caught their attention.

One of the
kits was
content to
sit there and
observe. The
second was
curious, but
was hiding
behind his
sibling and
wanted his
sibling to go
check it out
for him.

Maybe a
little push
would help.

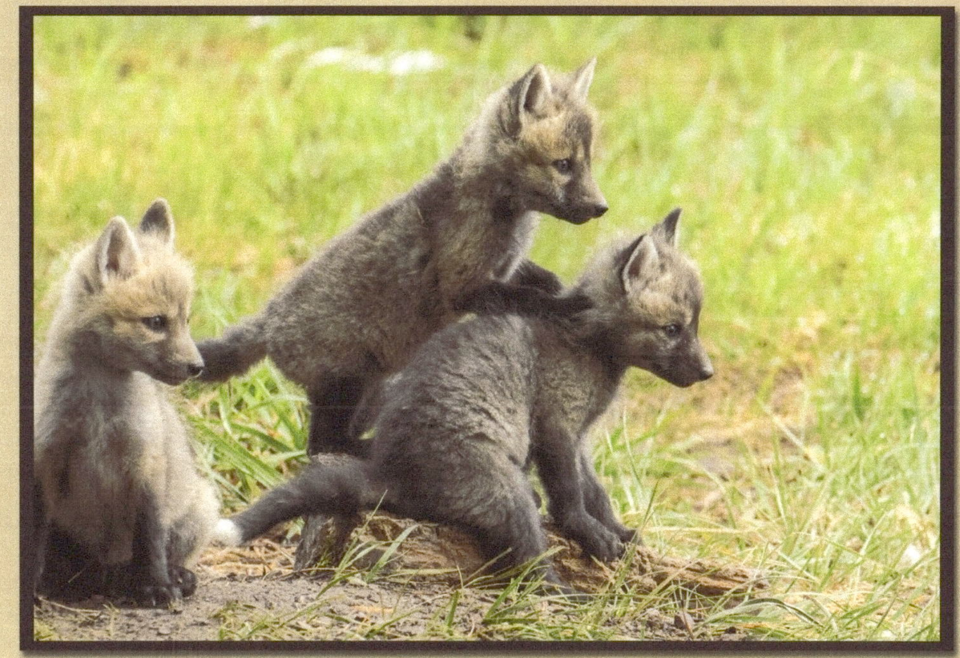

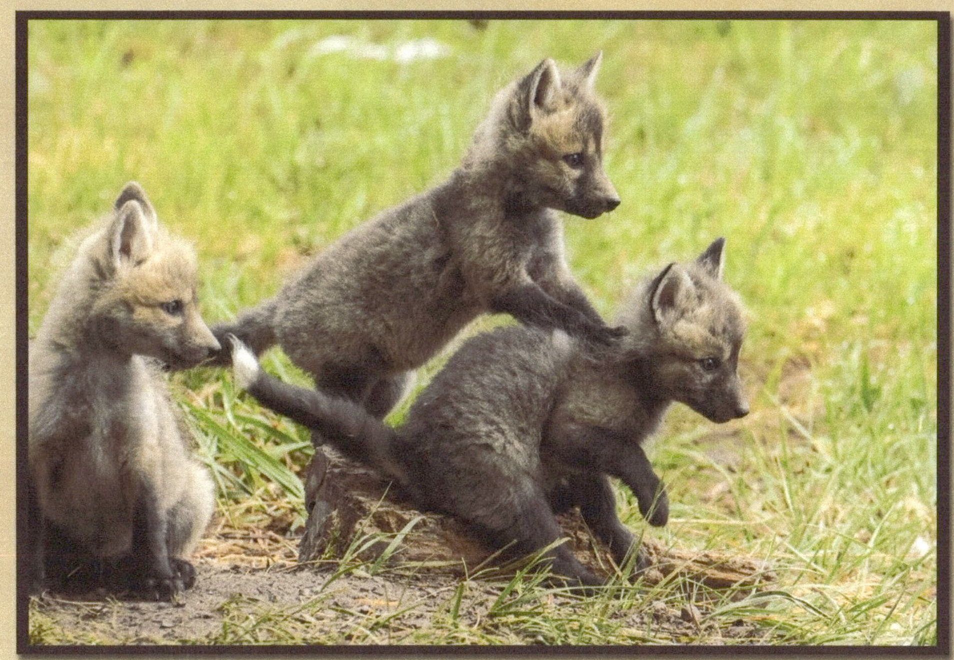

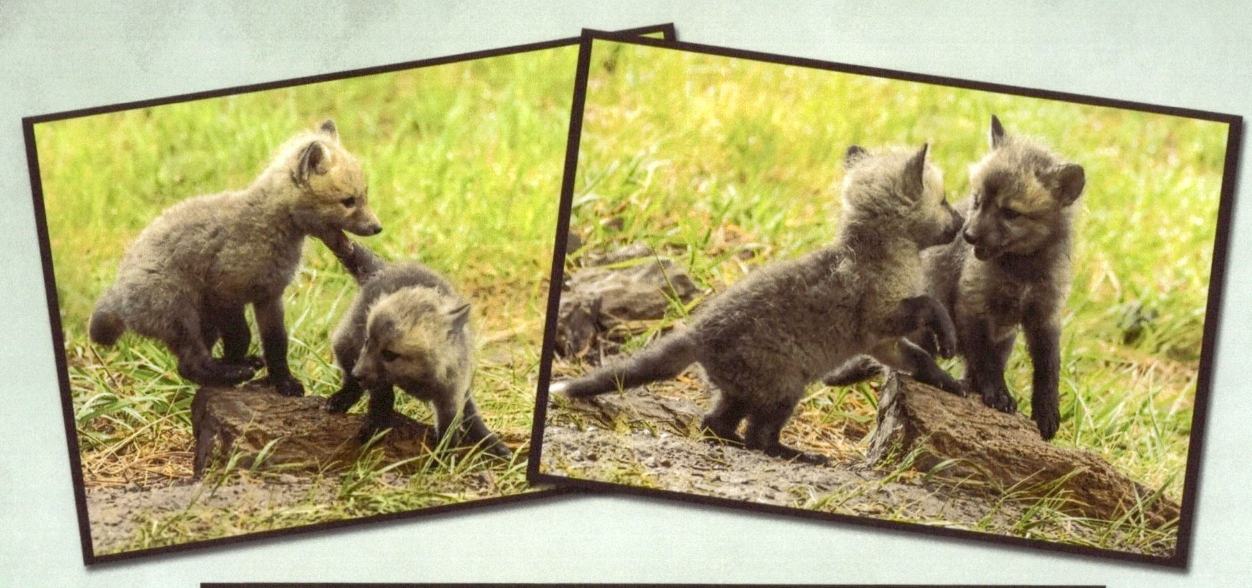

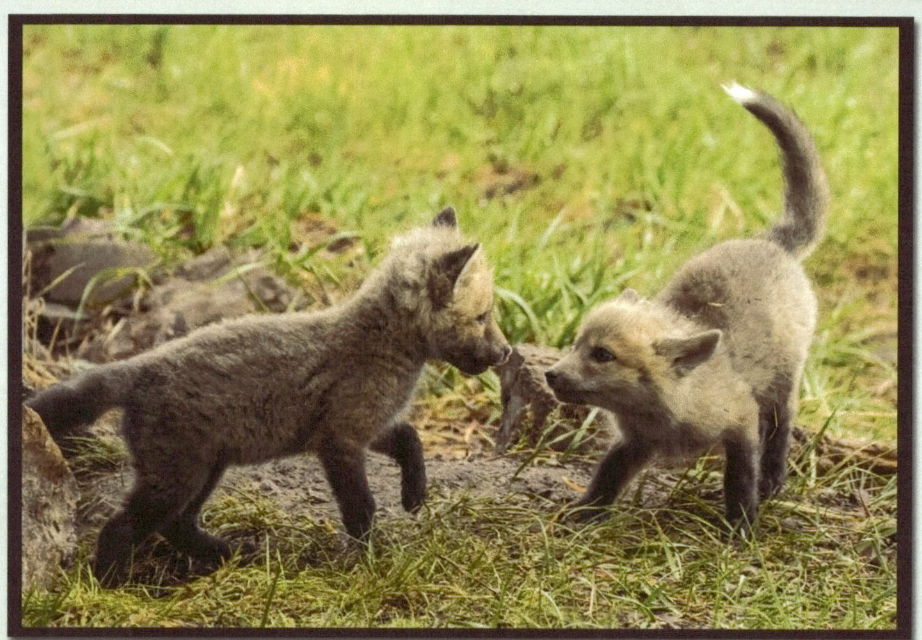

The kits seemed to instinctively know if you have the higher ground you have the advantage of the battle. Over time the kits became more ferocious. There seemed to be a growing competition in their play.

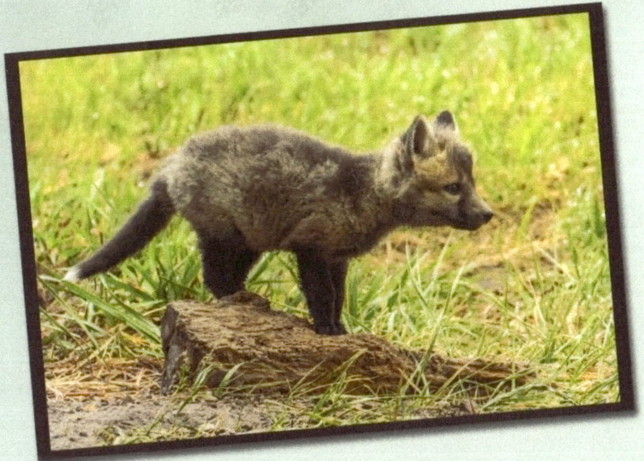 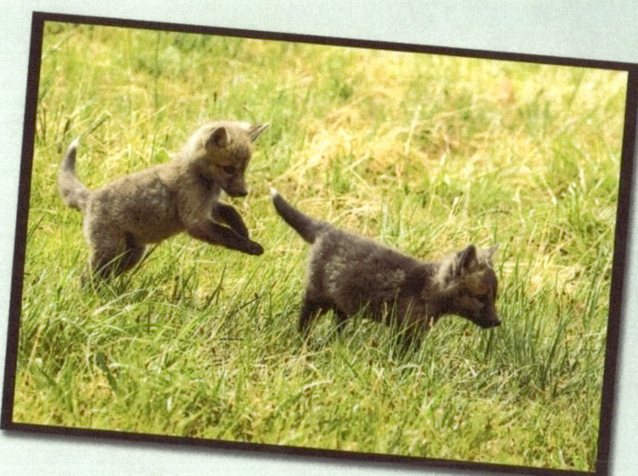

The fox diet consists mostly of mice, voles, lizards and small rabbits. It takes a lot of time to polish their skill of stalking the prey, but they start practicing early in life. The kit tries to get low to the ground and place his feet carefully so as not to make any noise that might give him away.

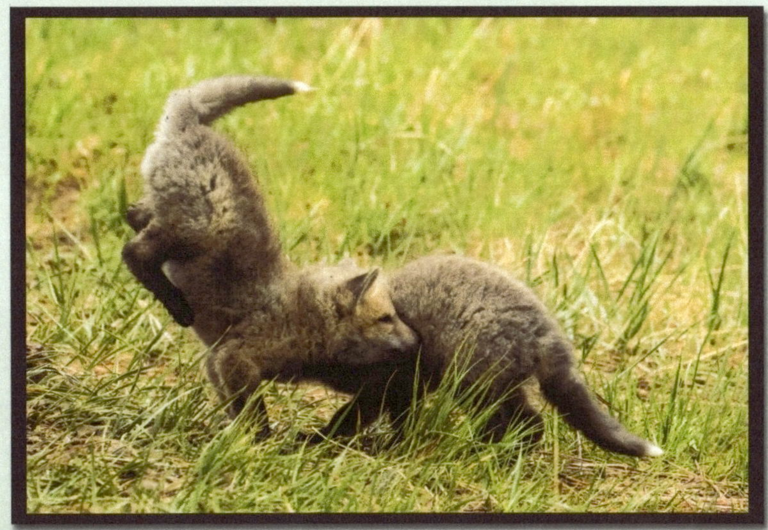

His ears are perked forward focusing on his prey and his eyes are locked on the target. His sibling does not know its tail is the target today. Sometimes the kit is not quiet enough and gets caught. Then it must make a sudden stop.

A strange noise? The snap of a twig? The cry of a kit?
Something is not right. You can see one ear turned
backward listening intently. The other ear is straight
forward listening in a different direction and you can
clearly see the look of fear in the vixen's eyes.

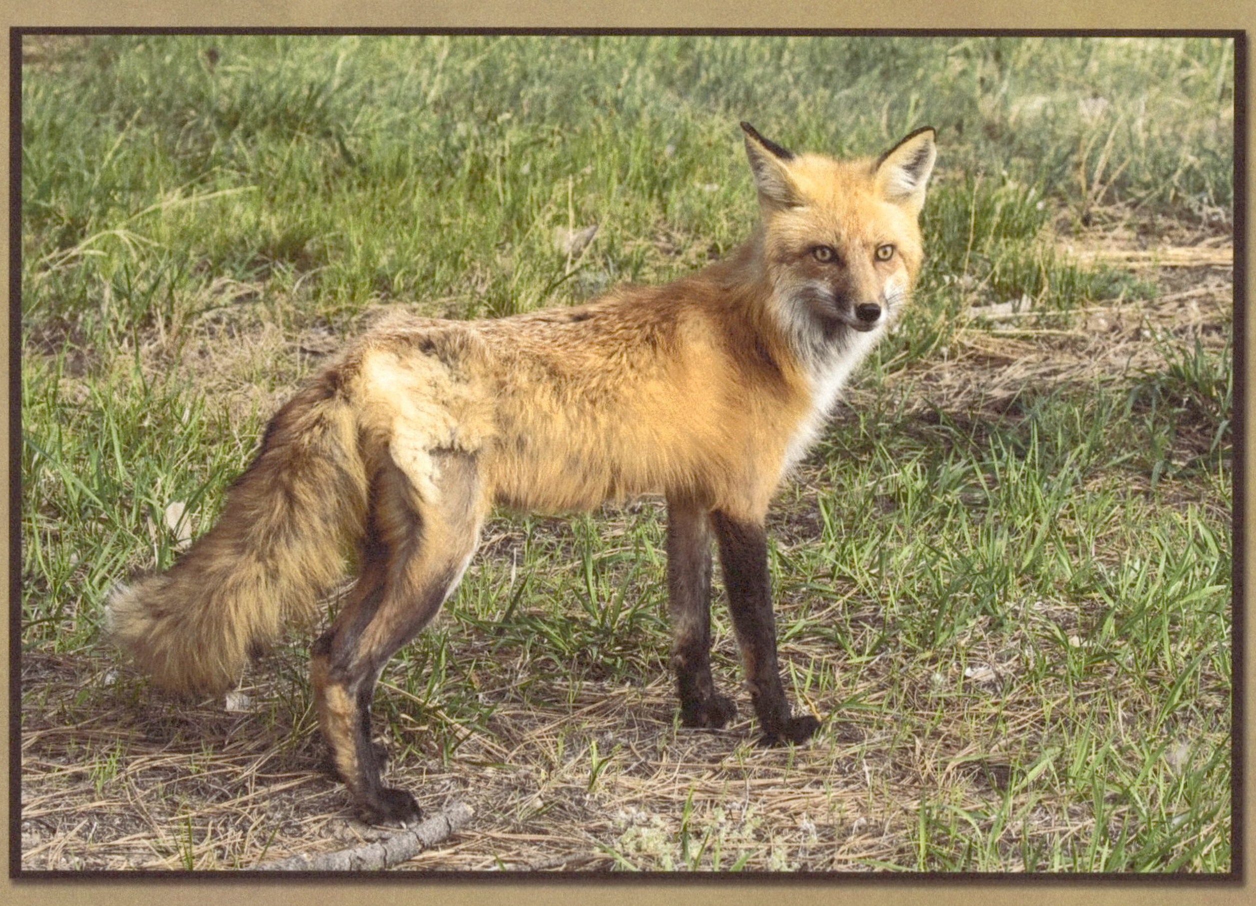

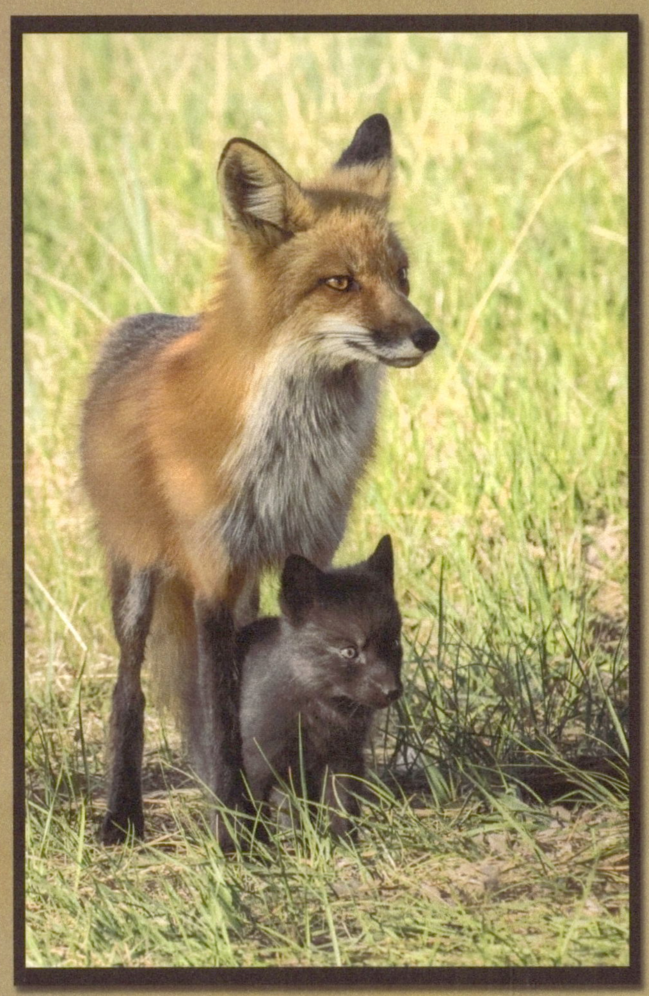

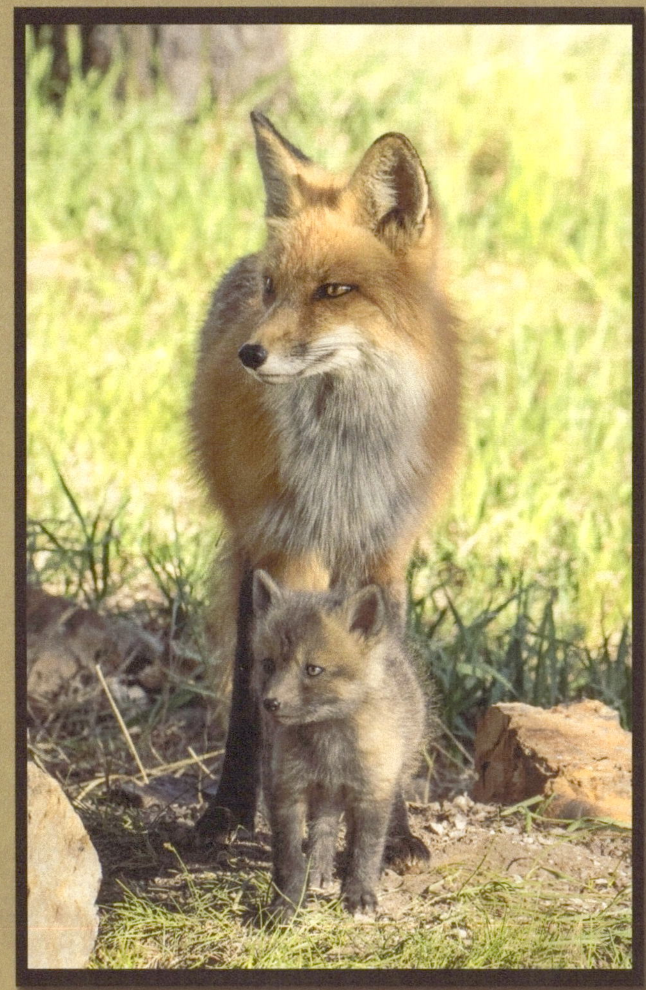

The vixen is teaching the
kits to search for danger.

I have heard that
animals in the wild
can identify their
young by their sense
of smell.

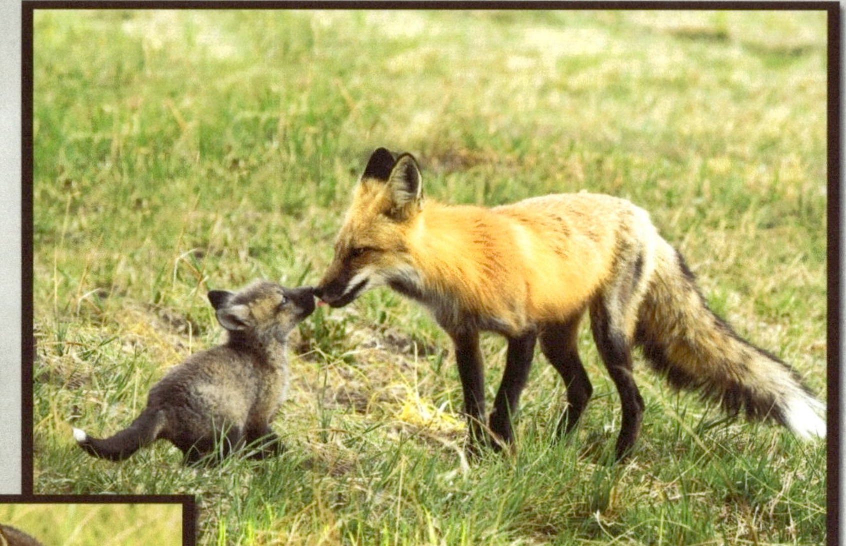

The kits were curious about
the vixen's breath when
she returned from a hunt.
This must be part of the
process of learning to hunt.

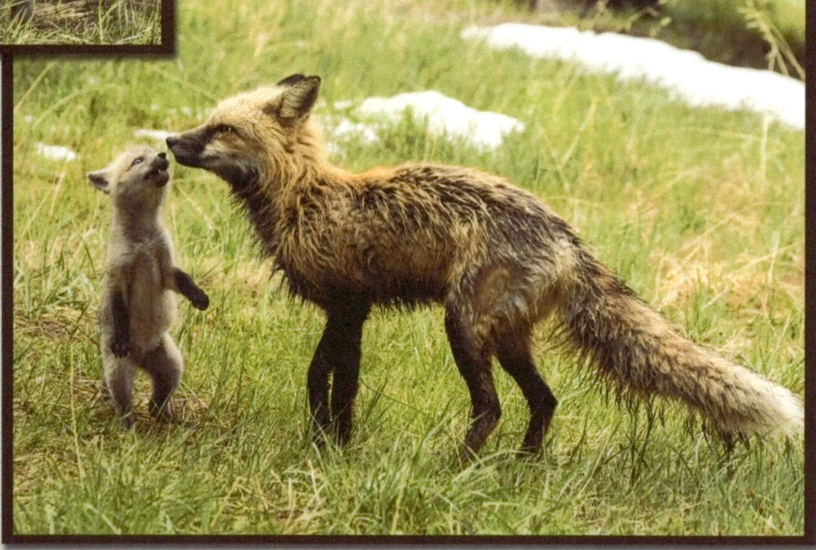

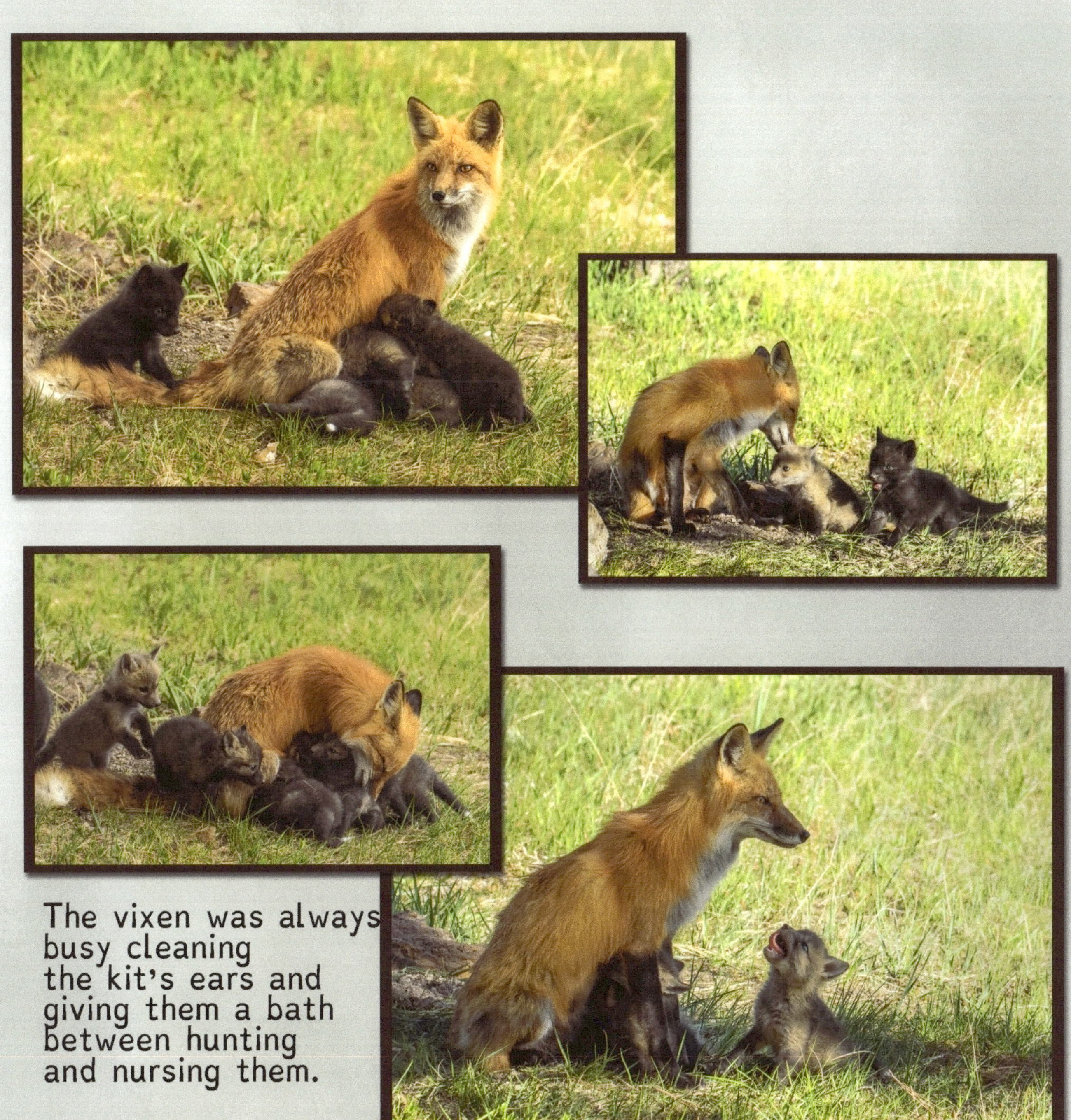

The vixen was always
busy cleaning
the kit's ears and
giving them a bath
between hunting
and nursing them.

The male fox was ever vigilant in guarding the den. So many times I arrived at the den and did not see anything, but after sitting there for a while and looking around I would discover him at some distance watching every movement in the area. He brought food to the vixen while she was confined to the den when the kits were so young she could not leave them. When the deer posed a threat, he was there to distract them and lead them away from the den.

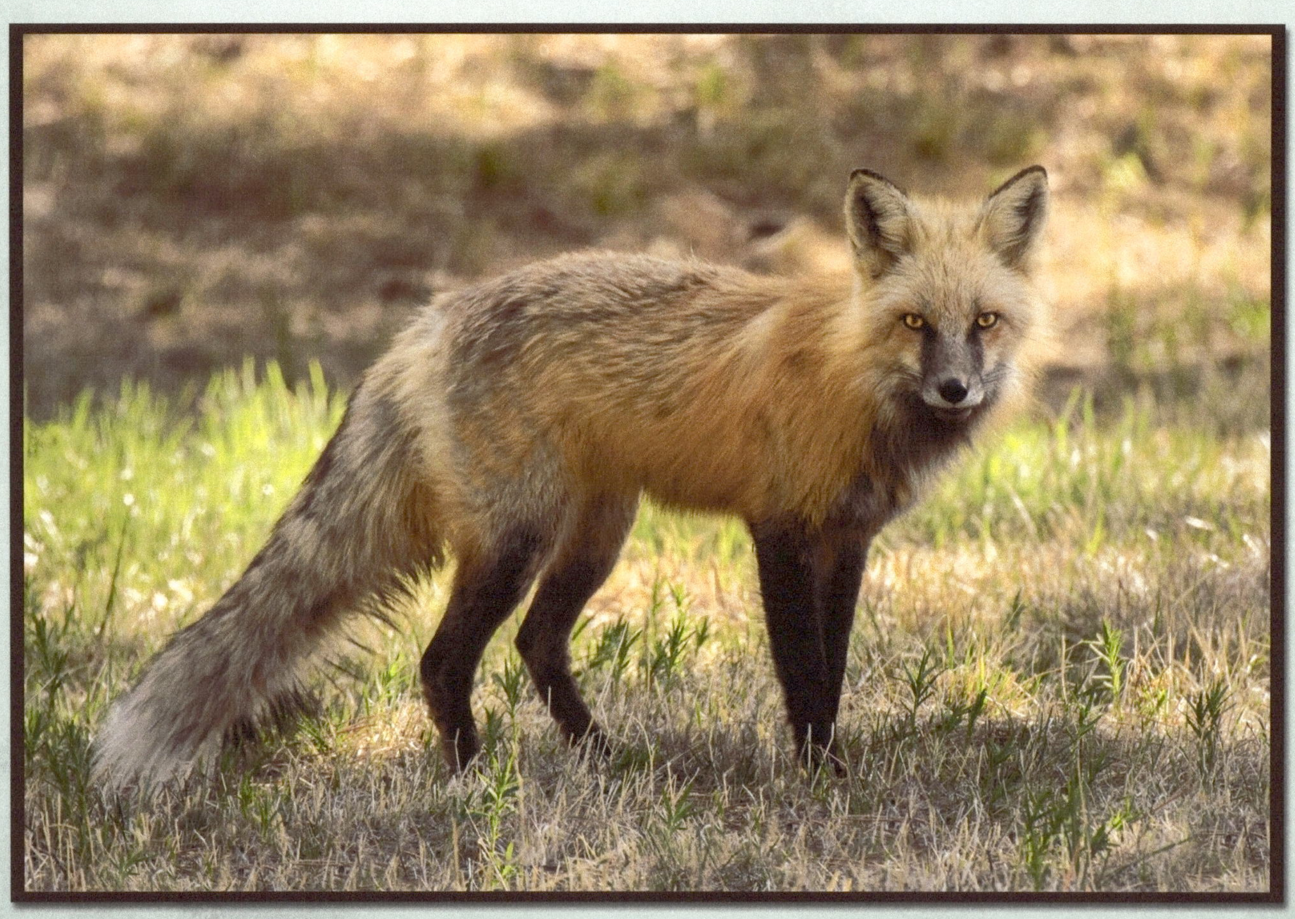

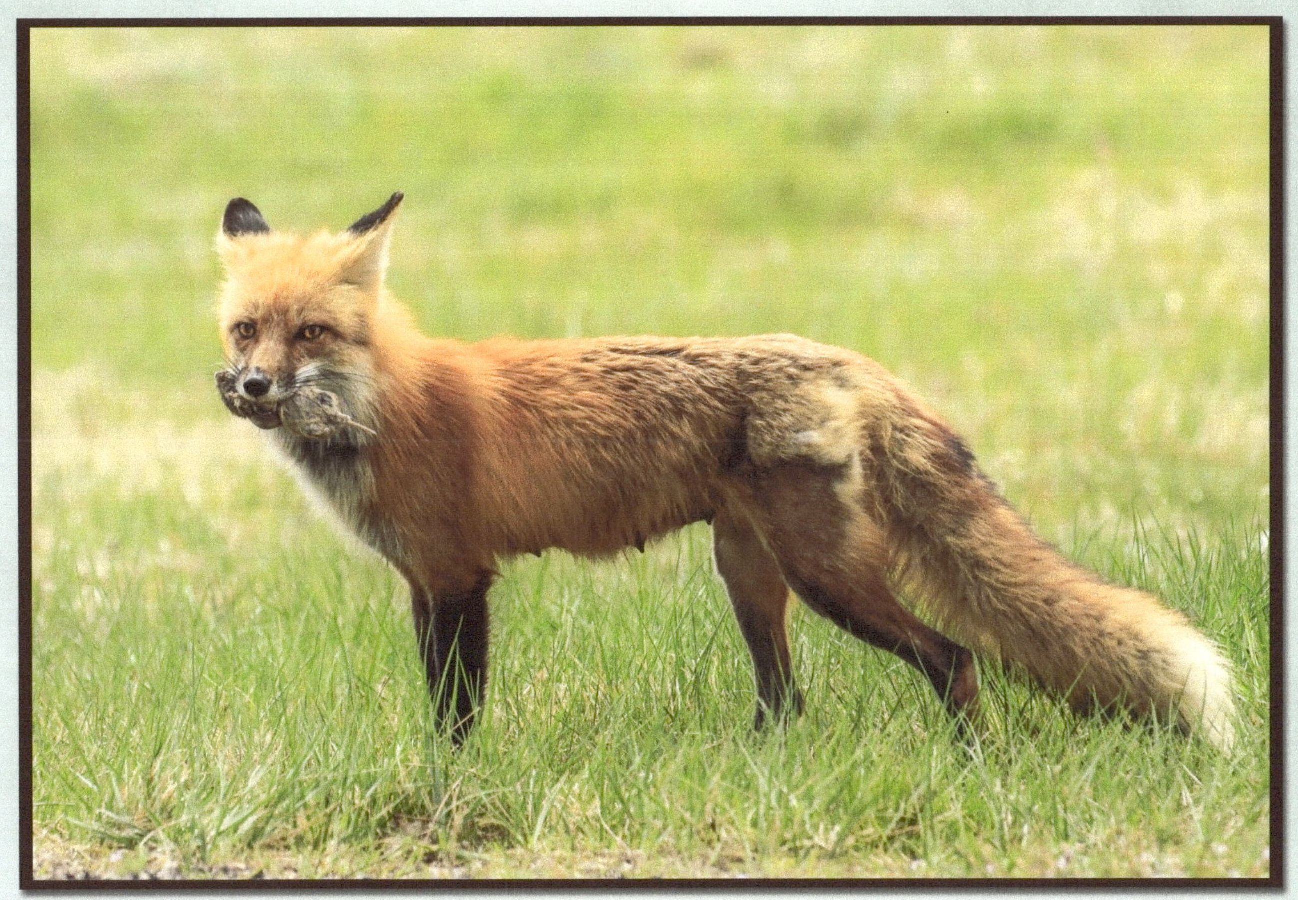

One afternoon the vixen had a vole in her mouth. She brought it to the den and called the kits out, but she would not give the vole to the kits. Instead she got just close enough for the kits to smell the vole. Then she turned and ran about twenty feet away from the den. The kits started to follow, but when they got about ten feet away from the den they turned around and ran back to the den. The vixen again brought the vole close to the kits to give them a sniff and then turned around and ran about twenty feet away from the den trying to get the kits to follow her. She must have done this at least twenty or more times. It appeared she was trying to coax the kits away from the den.

One day I saw the vixen coming to the den, but she did not have any food. She stopped at the south entrance to the den and announced her presence in that low guttural voice, but the kits did not come out. Instead, the vixen went into the den and after a few minutes she came out with a mouse in her mouth. She immediately headed north through the pasture into the pine trees until she disappeared out of sight. I waited until dark but she did not return. I knew something was different. I think the vixen moved the kits to a new den.

The more I watched the fox, the more I wanted to know about them so I did some research.

In Colorado, the fox mate in January or February. The gestation period is about fifty to fifty-two days and the kits are born in March or April. The kits do not come out of the den until they are about four weeks old and shortly thereafter they are eating solid food. During this time, the male will bring food to the den for the vixen.

The kits usually are weaned by ten weeks old. Although they are fully weaned, they still rely on their parents to provide food. The parents keep the kits at the birth den for the first several weeks and then they move to a new location. My friend, who is a biologist, told me it is believed that fox move their kits because the den becomes infested with parasites from the dead animals that they bring in for food. When the fox leaves the den, the parasites die. The fox has a series of dens and they may return to the same den once the parasites are gone. By twelve weeks the kits are exploring and hunting with their parents and by September or October they are looking for their own hunting territory.

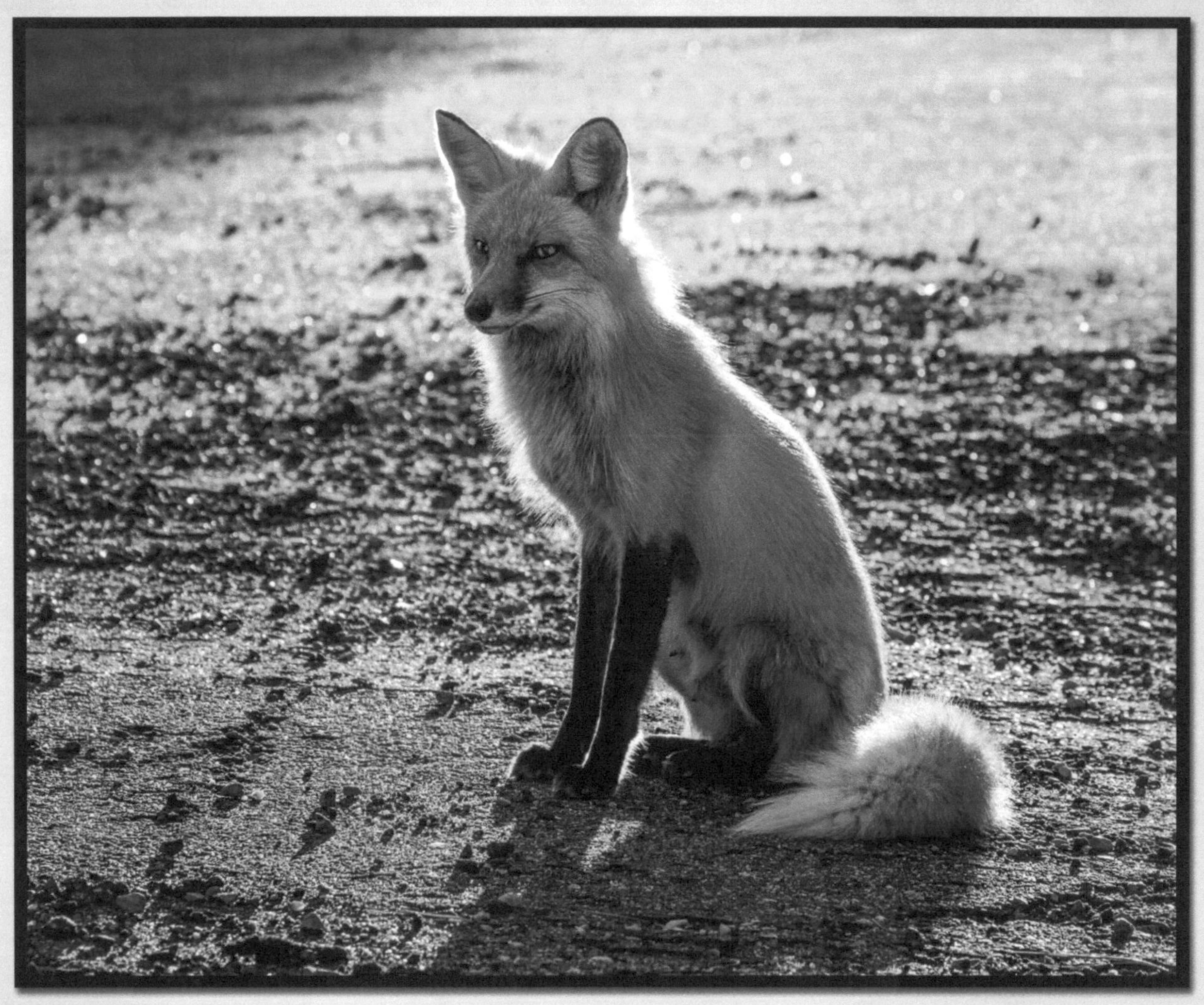

I had a lot of time to think about life and nature and behavior while watching the red fox, the kestrel, the red-tailed hawk, the mule deer, the squirrels and all the wildlife around me. I realized we have a lot in common with what we call "wild" life. We all have the same basic drive — the need to fight for survival, the need for food and water and the need to protect our young.

I will never forget my time with the red fox family. It was a wonderful time of contemplation and observation. It was a time to appreciate the beauty of God's creation. I am so glad I was able to capture it with my camera and share it with others.

I consciously and deliberately used the dyslexie font type to make it easier for people with dyslexia to read this book.

About the Author

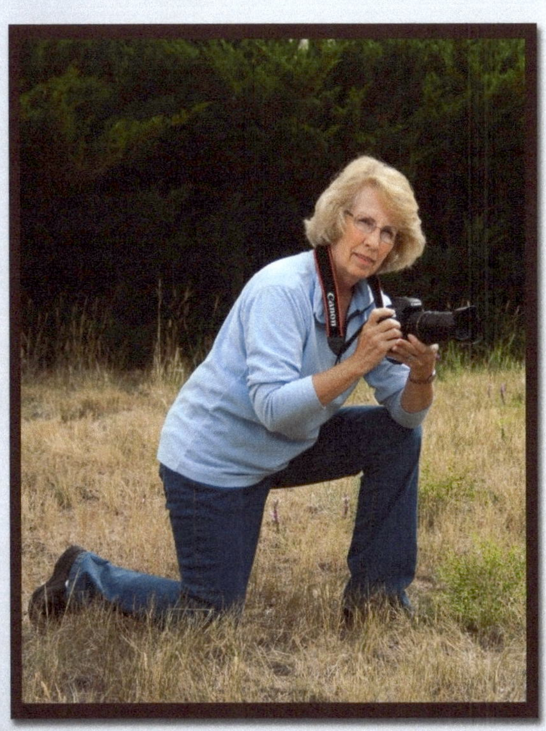

Lois grew up on a wheat farm on the great plains of Southeast Colorado. She discovered early that life is not always blue skies and sunshine, but it is full of opportunities. The key is to recognize those opportunities when they occur and take advantage of them. The skills of survival acquired on a farm and her resulting philosophy of life carries over into her photography. Lois likes to capture the stormy moods of nature and scenes of what happens in the outdoors. She is fascinated with non-verbal communication and body language, particularly among wildlife and enjoys the challenge of trying to capture that non-verbal communication in a photograph.

9 781943 650026